Looking at Vegetarianism

ISSUES

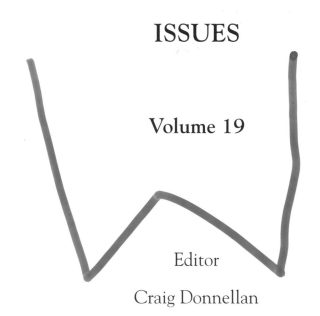

Volume 19

Editor

Craig Donnellan

Independence

Educational Publishers

Cambridge

First published by Independence
PO Box 295
Cambridge CB1 3XP
England

British Library Cataloguing in Publication Data
Looking at Vegetarianism – (Issues Series)
I. Donnellan, Craig II. Series
179.3

ISBN 1 86168 191 7

Printed in Great Britain
The Burlington Press
Cambridge

Typeset by
Claire Boyd

Cover
The illustration on the front cover is by
Pumpkin House.

CONTENTS

Chapter One: A Question of Diet

Vegetarian and vegan diets	1
Live and let live	2
The role of meat in a balanced diet	4
A few basic facts	6
Meat in the diet	8
Vegetarian nutrition	9
Meat and fat	10
How to be a vegetarian in ten easy steps	11
Vegan FAQs	12
Teen vegans	13
Nutrition or know your onions!	14
Eating for life	15
Farmers condemn anti-milk campaign aimed at children	17
The Dairy Council	18
Vegetarians offered discount offer	19
Vegetarians and heart disease	20
Cheat meat	21
Animal culls 'turning people into vegetarians'	22
Welcome return to pleasures of flesh	23

Chapter Two: Animal Welfare

Animal welfare	24
Go veggie	26
Animals and the environment	27
Freedom food	27
Suffering in silence	29
Meet your meat	30
Farm livestock – health and welfare	32
5 reasons for going veggie	33
Animal transport	34
Animal welfare	35
Progressive farmers	36
Factory farming	37
Egg-laying hens	38
Pig welfare	39
Pork adverts are banned in 'welfare friendly' row	40
Additional Resources	41
Index	42
Acknowledgements	44

Introduction

Looking at Vegetarianism is the nineteenth volume in the Issues series. The aim of this series is to offer up-to-date information about important issues in our world.

Looking at Vegetarianism examines the moral, ethical and dietary issues of vegetarianism and veganism and also looks at the issue of animal welfare.

The information comes from a wide variety of sources and includes:
Government reports and statistics
Newspaper reports and features
Magazine articles and surveys
Literature from lobby groups
and charitable organisations.

It is hoped that, as you read about the many aspects of the issues explored in this book, you will critically evaluate the information presented. It is important that you decide whether you are being presented with facts or opinions. Does the writer give a biased or an unbiased report? If an opinion is being expressed, do you agree with the writer?

Looking at Vegetarianism offers a useful starting-point for those who need convenient access to information about the many issues involved. However, it is only a starting-point. At the back of the book is a list of organisations which you may want to contact for further information.

*****

Vegetarian and vegan diets

Information from the British Nutrition Foundation (BNF)

BRITISH Nutrition FOUNDATION

Vegetarian diets range from simply avoiding red meat through to strict vegan diets.

In an omnivorous diet, animal foods normally provide substantial amounts of food energy, protein, calcium, iron, zinc, vitamins A, D and B12. A well-planned and varied vegetarian diet will provide adequate energy and nutrients but problems arise if those foods excluded are not replaced by suitable alternatives in terms of the nutrients they supply.

Many teenagers are adopting a vegetarian style of eating. These need to be well planned to ensure they provide the nutrients needed for growth and health. Such diets can be particularly problematic if they are also low in energy.

Special attention should be given to the iron intake of girls as iron deficiency anaemia is three times more common in vegetarian teenagers compared with non-vegetarians.

A vegetarian diet that maintains good health in adulthood may not necessarily be appropriate for infants and young children.

Research carried out in 1993 indicated that 4.3% of the population aged 16 and over do not eat meat and fish. This represented a total of two and a half million people. Young women are leading the way in the trend towards vegetarianism. In 1993, 13.3% of 16-24-year-old women, three times the national average, were vegetarian. However, vegetarianism is also increasing in men.

Types of vegetarian diets

Variations in strictness of vegetarianism are great and are largely dependent on the person's beliefs and reasons for adopting vegetarianism. This may be for a variety of personal, philosophical, ecological and economical reasons. Some understanding of these reasons is important when considering nutritional status.

'Semi' or 'demi' vegetarian

Exclusion of red meat or all meat, but fish and other animal products are still consumed; some people also exclude poultry

Lacto-ovo-vegetarian

Exclusion of all meat, fish and poultry; milk, milk products and eggs are still consumed

Lacto-vegetarian

Exclusion of all meat, fish and poultry and eggs; milk and milk products are still consumed

Vegan

Exclusion of all foods of animal origin; diets comprise vegetables, vegetable oils, cereals, pulses such as beans and lentils, nuts, fruit and seeds

Fruitarian

Exclusion of all foods of animal origin as well as pulses and cereals. Diets mainly comprise raw and dried fruits, nuts, honey and olive oil. People following this type of eating pattern are at great risk of nutritional deficiency; their diets require vitamin and mineral supplementation

Macrobiotic – sometimes referred to as Zen Macrobiotic diet

The diet progresses through a series of levels, gradually eliminating all animal produce, fruit and vegetables and leading to a restricted diet of cereal (brown rice) only. Fluids are also severely restricted. Children are particularly at risk of nutritional deficiency

• The above information is an extract from the British Nutrition Foundation's web site which can be found at www.nutrition.org.uk

© British Nutrition Foundation (BNF)

Live and let live

Information from Viva!

Going veggie isn't brain surgery – it's simple, sensible and safe. You're bound to have questions and whatever they are, we have the answers.

What is a veggie?

It's easier to say what vegetarians don't eat! No meat, fish or anything from a slaughterhouse such as gelatine and meat stocks. But vegetarians may eat dairy products and free-range eggs. A vegan avoids animal products entirely.

Ready, steady, cook

If you think about it – a lot of things in the store cupboard, fridge and freezer are veggie. You could walk into the kitchen right now and rustle up a great meal. There's fresh and frozen vegetables; pasta, rice and potatoes; tinned beans, tomatoes and sweet corn; flour, herbs and spices, noodles, oil and margarine. This alone will get you going but with a little bit of additional shopping, you're really in business.

All the old favourite foods are still on the agenda – pies and pasties, pizzas and paella, chilli and chunky chips, burgers and bangers, bacon and brilliant curries. The only difference is, there's no meat in them. It's obviously cheaper to cook these dishes yourself but ready-made versions are available everywhere. Supermarkets have a huge range but don't forget your local health food shop for good advice and really tasty alternatives.

Lazy daisy

If that's you then get down to your supermarket or health shop because there's all kinds of things in tins and packets – all you have to do is open them. There are pots of noodles, curries and chow mein, tins of spag bol, rigatoni and veggie ravioli. Pizzas, ratatouille, veg casserole with herb dumplings, stew – they're all there. And don't forget the humble baked bean – they even come with veggie sausages.

Viva!

Then there's nachos, refried beans and tortillas – not to mention garlic mushrooms, vegetable chilli, provençal and goulash. Eat them on their own or as toppings for baked potatoes.

Mighty meaty, matey

The last few years have seen a food revolution. Meat substitutes – usually made from soya or wheat protein – have been used to copy most of the traditional meat favourites. Dishes made from them are now the fastest selling food products of all.

So, if you still hanker after the taste or texture of meat, most supermarkets and health shops sell a wide range of these meat substitutes in the freezer or chiller section. There are grills and nuggets, sausages, 'meaty' pies, shepherd's pie, frankfurters and even very convincing bacon. If you're still cooking meat for others, some of these will go happily under the grill or in the oven at the same time.

Still one of the all-time favourites is burgers – and there are dozens of different veggie ones.

On stand by

All supermarkets have a big range of own-brand, ready-made vegetarian dishes either chilled or frozen. Health food shops tend to have a more unusual selection. Keep some at the ready in your freezer. Okay, so they're 'ping' meals but some are very good indeed – spinach roll, veggie spaghetti bolognese, mushroom stroganoff and dozens of others.

Gravy train

What do you do about sauces and gravies? Probably what you did before because there's vegetable stock cubes of every kind and most gravy brownings are veggie (check the labels). Add water from cooked veg, a splosh of olive oil, herbs and seasoning and you're in business.

Feel your pulse

Pulses – dried broad beans, butter beans, kidney beans, peas, lentils and so on are simple to use and highly nutritious. The tinned varieties are the most convenient as they just need to be heated but the dried ones, soaked and cooked, have more flavour. Add to any casserole or stew, turn them into wonderful patés and terrines or add chopped things (spring onions, garlic, herbs, coriander, parsley, red peppers and French dressing) to make great-tasting, nutritious salads.

Fancy foreigners

If 'meaty' meals don't appeal then look at the countries who have a tradition of vegetarian cookery – Italy, India, Thailand, Turkey. Get a good cookery book or two and start to live. You'll be spoilt for choice. Call Viva! on 01273 777688 for a free book catalogue.

Out and about

If you think that eating out will be a disaster – it won't. Just about every restaurant in the country offers a veggie choice – some a big one. And the number of dedicated vegetarian/vegan restaurants is growing all the time.

Many traditional Italian dishes are vegetarian anyway – parmigiano (aubergines), pesto, Napolitana (tomato sauce), arabiatta (tomato with chilli) and spinach & veg served in pasta parcels. And of course, there are pizzas galore (choose a veggie or vegan topping). Don't be afraid to ask what's vegetarian if it's not marked.

Indian restaurants have some great vegetarian dishes but often they're called 'side dishes' – aloo gobi (potatoes and cauliflower), tarka dhall (lentils with garlic), brinjal bhaji (curried aubergines), vegetable balti, bindi bhaji (okra curry). If you can find a South Indian place, almost everything will be veggie.

Greek and Turkish restaurants can often have a good choice of dishes listed under 'mezzes'. Some Chinese aren't bad either – ask what's veggie – usually there's everything from veg chow mein to veg sweet 'n' sour. Thai can be excellent – try a dish such as potato and peanut curry in coconut sauce with ginger or garlic rice.

Healthy and happy

What's so important about meat? Not a lot, really! It plays a big part in causing cancers, heart disease, strokes, high blood pressure, diet-related diabetes, gall stones and other diseases. Most vegetarians are healthier than meat eaters and live longer. No argument, no dispute – it's a simple statement of fact. Giving up meat is one of the most sensible things you can do. And what do you risk by dumping meat – absolutely nothing!

The three things in meat you don't need are saturated fat, cholesterol and animal protein. There is less of all these in the average veggie diet. Those that are there come mostly from dairy products. The fewer animal products you eat, the healthier you are likely to be.

Food poisoning is a massive problem and new strains of bacteria have become resistant to antibiotics. More than 95 per cent of food poisoning comes from animal products so avoiding them cuts your risk.

Health is a covered at length in Viva!'s guide, *The Healthiest Diet of All*. Written by Dr David Ryde MRCGP, it's easy to read and has more than 130 scientific references and costs £1.50 (inc. p&p).

> 'You don't need anyone's permission to go veggie! Do it and help to end cruelty to animals, help the environment, give a boost to the world's starving and improve your health.'
> Paul McCartney

Nutrition for novices

A good vegetarian diet – based

> 'Because I'm vegan, I'm happier knowing that my actions have not caused the direct suffering of other creatures.'
> Moby – musician

> 'Viva! has grown rapidly from nothing and it is now making real changes – to the way people think about animals and what they choose to eat. I'm right behind them.'
> Joanna Lumley – actress

around complex carbohydrates such as potatoes, pasta, rice and other starchy foods, with a good mix of fresh fruit and veg, grains and pulses and some seeds and nuts – provides you with more of all the nutrients you need and less of those you don't need. Whole foods such as brown rice and wholemeal bread are far more nutritious than the processed, white varieties.

Far from being a great source of nutrients, meat is seriously lacking. There's no fibre, calcium or complex carbohydrates and there's no (or very little) vitamins A (betacarotene), C, E, D or K in meat. A (betacarotene), C, and E are the vital antioxidant vitamins that protect you against disease – and they are found almost exclusively in fresh fruit and veg. As for warnings of iron deficiency – it's no more likely to afflict a veggie than a meat eater. However, it's important for everyone to have iron-rich foods in their diet – green leafy veg, baked beans, dried fruit, cocoa and lentils are good sources. As for protein – vegetarians get more than enough.

If you want to know more, send for Viva!'s guide, *Nutrition in a Nutshell*. Written by nutritionist Dr Chris Fenn and edited by Michael Klaper MD, it costs £1 (inc. p&p).

The strongest link

Q: Is it healthy?
A: Yes – very.

Q: Will I get the right nutrients?
A: Yes – plenty.

Q: Where will I get protein?
A: In almost everything you eat.

Q: Does age matter?
A: Not a bit.

Q: Isn't it a 'second class' diet?
A: No – it's the best.

Q: Am I more likely to become anaemic?
A: No.

Q: What will I eat?
A: Masses of good things.

> 'When it comes to vegetarian food – count me in. With such great flavours and so much choice, it's a wonderful life!'
> Emma Wray – actress, *Watching*, *Stay Lucky*, *My Wonderful Life*

You'll find plenty more ideas in Viva!'s *L-Plate Vegetarian* and *L-Plate Vegan* – 36-page guides to going veggie or vegan. They cost £1.50 (inc. p&p) each.

If it's recipes you're after, Viva! patron Pam 'Ma Larkin' Ferris has written a 28-page starter guide for just this occasion. Great recipes and cookery tips to take you from breakfast to dinner time. Just £1.50 (inc. p&p).

> 'There was once a vegan called Steven, Who just would not kill for no reason. He would not eat cheese and not eat meat And hated the fox hunting season . . .'
> 'I'm right behind Viva!'
> Benjamin Zephaniah – poet and Viva! patron

> 'Being vegetarian has nothing to do with austerity – I use the best of everything. But it's about principles as well. I feel strongly that I could never hurt an animal and now I don't have to!'
> Pam Ferris – actress and Viva! patron

• The above information is from an information leaflet produced by Viva! See their web site at www.viva.org.uk or e-mail at info@viva.org.uk Alternatively, see page 41 for their address details.
© Viva!

The role of meat in a balanced diet

Information from the Meat and Livestock Commission (MLC)

What is the Meat and Livestock Commission?

The Meat and Livestock Commission was set up by an act of Parliament in 1967 to improve the efficiency of the meat and livestock industries and to encourage greater responsiveness to consumer needs. It is known to consumers through the brand 'British Meat'. This is regularly featured on television with 'The Recipe for Love' advertisements and in numerous promotions with supermarkets and butchers to encourage the sale of British beef, pork and lamb.

In addition, the British Meat Nutrition Education Service provides healthcare professional with a range of education materials and services to aid their role in giving dietary information to the public, Their team of qualified Dieticians, Nutritionists and Regional Education and Health Sector Managers offers expert advice on food and nutrition issues.

Health strategies for England, Scotland and Wales

In 1999 the new health strategies for England, Scotland and Wales were published: 'Saving Lives: Our Healthier Nation', 'Towards a Healthier Scotland' and 'Better Health: Better Wales'. Although written specifically for their country, there are some common threads that run through all three. There is recognition that social, economic and environmental circumstances, as well as lifestyle factors and individual choices, influence health. They also call for an integrated approach and collaborative working between Government, local and national organisations and individuals themselves. This is something in which the British Meat Nutrition Education Service is actively involved.

What is healthy eating or a healthy diet?

The Government's advice for a healthy diet is still based on the targets set out in the health strategies of the early 90s, e.g. the 1996 Scottish Diet Action Plan, in which it states 'lean cuts of meat must be chosen, trimmed of visible fat before cooking'. It also echoes the 1994 Committee on Medical Aspects of Food Policy (COMA) report on cardiovascular disease, in which nutritional targets were put into the context of actual food consumed. According to this COMA report, there is no need to reduce intakes of meat, just to switch to leaner cuts, or trim visible fat.

This is also reflected in the COMA report (1998) on diet and cancer, which recommends that those whose red meat intake is below the average should not reduce their intake, and that all recommendations should be in the context of a balanced diet.

They all suggest that a healthy diet includes a wide variety of foods taken from the four main food groups: bread, other cereals and potatoes; fruit and vegetables; meat, fish and alternatives; milk and dairy foods. Foods containing fats and sugars are also an integral part of a balanced diet, but are needed in very small amounts.

It is important that food should be enjoyable as well as nutritious. It is easily possible to make many different dietary choices which all fit within the Government reports. Everyone must therefore relate the advice and recommendations that are given, to their individual diet, lifestyle and health status.

Man's evolution as a meat eater

Some 97 per cent of British consumers eat meat (Taylor Nelson

---

UK meat industry data

Consumption of meat in the United Kingdom (Kg). These figures are based on estimated supplies of each meat on a carcase weight basis, divided by the mid-year population figure for the UK. This includes retail sales, processed meat sales and sales of each meat in the foodservice sector. The figures exclude imports of processed meat products such as corned beef, patés etc.

	1995	1996	1997	1998	1999	2000	2001
Beef and veal	15.4	12.6	14.4	15.0	15.4	16.0	15.3
Mutton and lamb	6.0	6.2	5.9	6.5	6.4	6.5	5.9
Pork	12.8	13.3	14.0	14.3	13.8	13.3	13.0
Bacon	8.0	8.0	7.8	8.0	7.9	7.7	7.6
Poultry meat	25.3	26.9	26.4	27.8	28.5	28.6	28.7
Total meat	67.4	67.1	68.7	71.6	72.0	72.1	70.5

© Meat and Livestock Commission (MLC)

Family Food Panel 1998) with an average red meat and processed meat consumption of 90g per person per day (Department of Health, 1998). It is therefore a major component of the diet. To the consumer, meat is versatile, convenient, good value and enjoyable. It is a food commodity that has served us well throughout human evolution.

Anthropological research suggest that if man had not eaten we may not have developed as we are. There is a relationship between diet, brain size and gut size. A paper by Aiello & Wheeler (1995) argued that selection for relatively large brains in humans could not have been achieved without a move to a higher quality diet, based on animal products.

The red meats (beef, lamb and pork) have a high nutrient density. In other words they contain a wide variety of nutrients in useful amounts. Meat is a major source of protein. It is also an important source of B vitamins, including B12, which is not found naturally in foods of plant origin. Meat also contributes minerals and trace elements to the diet, particularly iron and zinc. No one food contains all the nutrients needed for good health. The aim should be to include a wide variety of foods in the diet.

Meat and Iron

Iron is a vital mineral for red blood cell formation. A deficiency of iron in the diet is the most common dietary cause of anaemia. Evidence is now strong that there is a major problem of iron deficiency in the British diet. Certain groups of the population are particularly at risk because of poor iron intakes.

The National Diet and Nutrition Survey: Children Aged 1½ to 4½ Years (Gregory et al, 1995) found that 1 in 12 of all children and 1 in 8 of the younger age group were anaemic with another study showing 23% of 8-month-old infants to be anaemic (Emond et al, 1996), using the World Health Organisation (WHO) indicator of anaemia as a haemoglobin concentration below 11.0g/dl. Iron deficiency is the most commonly reported nutritional disorder reported during early childhood.

Food survey

TNS Family Food Panel comprises a representative panel of 11,000 individuals in 4,200 households. A diary of their eating and drinking is completed for two weeks in every 6 months. The diaries show that:

5.8% claim to be vegetarian but of these:

	%
Eat meat and fish	86.3%
Eat red meat, bacon and sausages	69.4%
Eat sausages	55.1%
Eat fish	52.9%
Eat red meat	26.6%

% 0 20 40 60 80 100

In the population as a whole:

	%
Eat red meat, poultry, bacon and sausages	97%
Eat red meat and poultry	94%
Eat poultry	84%
Eat red meat	79%

% 0 20 40 60 80 100

Source: Meat and Livestock Commission (MLC)

Furthermore using the WHO indicator of a ferritin level of below 10 mcg/l to indicate low iron stores, and hence iron deficiency, 1 in 5 children overall could be classed as iron deficient.

The COMA report *Weaning and the Weaning Diet* (Department of Health, 1994) stated 'It is a matter of concern that diets commonly used during weaning may provide inadequate absorbable iron.' The report suggest that 'well cooked, puréed meat' should be introduced during the initial 4 to 6 months stage of the weaning process and that foods containing haem iron should be introduced by 6 to 8 months. In other words, meat can be introduced in the early stages of weaning and should be part of the diet of a 6 to 8-month-old baby (unless the infant is being weaned on to a meat-free diet). It is not just babies and young children that are at risk of developing iron deficiency leading to anaemia, but also rapidly growing teenagers, the elderly, women with heavy periods and people who stop eating meat

without thinking about what should take its place.

In the latest *National Diet and Nutrition Survey* (Gregory et al 2000), a high proportion of young people aged 4 to 18 years were found to have iron intakes below the recommended amount (RNI), particularly in the older girls. Whilst intakes below the RNI do not necessarily indicate iron deficiency, they could mean that individuals may be entering their adult years at risk of anaemia. These vulnerable groups should at least be made aware of the relationship between lean meat and iron intake if they are choosing not to eat meat. Iron deficiency is a common problem in women. Indeed one study showed that 1 in 3 women have been found to be iron deficient in this country (White et al, 1993) and in a review of all the relevant research, up to 43% of British adolescent girls had low iron stores (Nelson, 1996). Red meat as part of a balanced diet is one way to improve iron intakes.

The COMA report *Dietary Reference Values for Food Energy and Nutrients for the United Kingdom* (1991) cautioned that iron in diets containing little or no meats is less well absorbed and that people habitually consuming such diets may need a higher iron intake.

This illustrates what can happen if dietary messages are too simplistic, e.g. the simple advice is to cut down on fat intake. The practical application of this is to cut out foods which contribute fat in the diet. In the past this has been interpreted as a need to cut down on red meat and dairy foods. There are, however, many sources of fat in the diet, and the importance of each varies with an individual's own dietary preferences. As a consequence, the national diet is now lower in iron and calcium, as well as fat. Choosing lean red meat would help to ensure that fat intakes remain at a lower level, but would help to maintain iron intakes.

• The above is an extract from *MeatMatters – information for Health Professionals*, produced by the Meat and Livestock Commission. See page 41 for their address details.

© *Meat and Livestock Commission (MLC)*

A few basic facts

There are many myths and prejudices that surround vegetarianism, but what exactly is the truth? What is a vegetarian, why do people give up flesh foods and what exactly is at stake? Information from the Vegetarian Society

What is a vegetarian?

Someone who eats no meat, poultry, game or fish, and who also avoids slaughterhouse by-products such as gelatine, rennet (an enzyme from a calf's stomach sometimes found in cheese) and animal fats.

Most vegetarians in the UK eat dairy produce and free-range eggs – they are referred to as lacto-ovo vegetarians. The Vegetarian Society only approves free-range eggs which are produced to standards above and beyond EU criteria for free-range egg farming. The Society believes that hens are more likely to behave naturally and remain healthy under such conditions.

Vegans avoid all animal products, including dairy produce, eggs and even honey.

Who are vegetarians?

Vegetarians are a diverse group of people of all ages, who come from all over the UK – from every walk of life imaginable. That includes people like YOU.

Far from being old-fashioned, faddy or eccentric, a vegetarian diet is the choice of many millions of people in search of healthy, delicious, cruelty-free food.

It is fair to say that the vast majority of people in the UK, most of the time, eat foods which either are, or could easily be, vegetarian. If you consider a traditional Sunday roast for instance, most of the food on the plate consists of vegetables anyway.

More people than ever are turning away from traditional meat and fish-based meals in search of something more satisfying.

But why go vegetarian?

Modern vegetarian food is far more accessible and diverse than it has ever been. Mouthwatering, satisfying veggie food is now available almost everywhere – and this is just one of

the reasons why it has never been easier to go vegetarian.

It is also true to say that many people have become bored with the limitations offered by traditional flesh-based foods, craving something that is fresh, exciting and very often different.

Vegetarian food offers this and so much more.

Although vegetarian food tastes fantastic and offers a wide scope of choice and flavour, in many cases it is also cheaper than meat and fish-based meals. It is neither hard to find nor difficult to prepare, but the fact remains that most people in the UK adopting a vegetarian diet do so out of concern for animal welfare, the environment and their own health.

Better for animals

In the UK alone, almost 800 million animals are slaughtered for food each

year. That means about fifteen live animals, per person, per year.

These animals are as intelligent and feeling as any household pet. Yet mostly they are intensively reared, forced to live tortured, short and miserable lives; denied access to their young and deprived of any real quality of life; fed unnatural diets, in some cases pumped full of chemicals to improve yield and lessen disease; kept in cramped conditions where they frequently develop physical and psychological abnormalities.

Then they are transported from factory farm to livestock market and finally to the horrors of the slaughterhouse.

Some animals even have to endure the long, stressful and hazardous haul to markets abroad, often in extremes of weather, without adequate provision of food, water, air and light, to places where conditions are often much worse.

Then they are finally put out of their misery in the most barbaric manner.

Without doubt, the greatest single cause of animal suffering in the UK is food production. Vegetarianism is the only humane and civilised answer.

Better for the environment

A vegetarian diet is much better for the environment and meat and fish production is without doubt contributing to damaging our planet irreparably.

Methane-emitting livestock contribute to global warming and the 'Greenhouse Effect' – roughly about one-quarter of all methane emissions come from this source. Ammonia from animal waste and agricultural fertilisers contributes to acid rain, which kills aquatic and plant life. Intensive grazing causes soil erosion and nutrient depletion, which harms plant life and in some cases renders the soil infertile, creating vast, barren deserts where previously there was fertile land.

Livestock cultivation makes inefficient use of limited resources. It takes up to ten kilos of vegetable protein to produce just one kilo of meat. While it takes only 900 litres of water to produce 1 kilo of wheat an incredible 100,000 litres are needed to produce a single kilo of meat.

Clean and safe water is not an inexhaustible resource and it is becoming ever more scarce. Yet in certain cases, people in the developing world go hungry and thirsty while grain and water is squandered on rearing animals for food, often destined for markets in the developed world.

In the UK meat production takes care of 150 billion litres of water each year. In terms of land usage, the UK alone is capable of feeding 250 million people with a healthy, nutritious and affordable vegetarian diet all year round.

Millions of hectares of life-sustaining rain forest have been destroyed to create grazing pasture, with the meat produced destined in part for the developed world.

This recklessness goes on and is responsible for killing and endangering rapidly disappearing animal and bird species. Such operations also threaten indigenous human populations, whose long-established ways of living vanish or become damaged for ever.

The extent to which the world's oceans are fished has decimated fish populations to the point of near extinction of many species. The world's seas are being fished to the point of collapse and in the North Sea alone, cod and herring numbers are now at dangerously low levels.

This is despite the fact that some of the world's seas close to industrialised areas contain potentially lethal cocktails of toxic waste and effluent some of the results of which can be seen in the open sores, cancerous tumours and deformities found on some captured fish.

The fragile eco-systems of the world's oceans continue to be ruined and coral reefs and other habitats are being destroyed. Pollution and fishing are two of the major causes.

Research has also shown that a vegetarian diet could help reduce risks from certain cancers by up to 40 per cent

Dolphins, whales, sharks and turtles are also indiscriminately killed by drift netting and in some parts of the world, such species are still deliberately slaughtered for food.

Massive amounts of dead and dying fish are thrown back into the sea, ironically deemed too small, they are needlessly deprived of life, as factory fishing vessels lay waste vast areas of the sea in minutes. Such needless destruction means that not enough numbers are reaching suitable maturity to replenish the species properly.

Not content with destroying marine life in the natural environment, intensive farming techniques have been introduced to 'cultivate' fish. This practice is called aquaculture and is responsible for 10 per cent of current global fish sources, with this figure set to rise as natural stocks become dangerously depleted.

Instinctively migratory species, such as salmon and trout, are caged up in very close confines and forced to live unnatural, short lives, with high premature mortality and even cannibalism all too evident. Such fish are fed large doses of chemicals, as disease and infection can be rife. They are then slaughtered after about 14 months of life.

The list goes on and the crimes against the environment are many. Far more people are now becoming aware that a vegetarian diet makes far better use of the world's resources and is a positive way of contributing to the future well-being of the planet.

Vegetarian food will not cost you the Earth.

Better for health

Research has shown that a well-balanced, low-fat, high-fibre vegetarian diet is a very healthy option and vegetarians certainly need not go short of any nutrients, vitamins or minerals.

In recent years people have been forced to think much more about the health implications of the food on their plates. This is in light of recent health scares such as E-coli and, of course, BSE ('Mad Cow Disease') and nvCJD (the deadly human form), which resulted in the widespread banning of British beef, with billions of pounds of public money wasted and millions of innocent animals slaughtered.

Research has also shown that a vegetarian diet could help reduce risks from certain cancers by up to 40 per cent; decrease the possibility of dying from heart disease by 30 per cent; restrict the chance of suffering from kidney and gall stones, diet-related diabetes and even high blood pressure. It could also lower cholesterol levels and reduce health problems related to obesity. Over 90 per cent of all food poisoning cases each year in the UK are related to the consumption of animal products.

What about GMOs?

There is currently a widespread unease concerning the possible future implications and effects of the proliferation and wider application of gene technology, particularly with regard to food.

Amongst many other organisations and individuals, the Vegetarian Society believes that insufficient research has been carried out into the potential environmental and health implications of genetic manipulation, and the Society is concerned that the introduction of Genetically Modified (GM) foods could cause risk to the environment, animal welfare and human health.

In addition, the extensive animal experimentation undertaken during the development of these synthetically altered natural forms of plant life is contrary to the Society's principles.

In all of these areas, the Vegetarian Society is campaigning hard, promoting the very many benefits of vegetarianism, to push for change and create a better world through the food on our plates.

• The above information is an extract from the Vegetarian Society's web site which can be found at www.vegsoc.org

Meat in the diet

Information from the British Nutrition Foundation (BNF)

1. The majority of people in the UK eat meat. When meat is eaten, it should be lean and part of a balanced and varied diet which is based on fruit, vegetables and carbohydrate foods such as potatoes, bread, rice and pasta.

2. Lean meat is a nutritious food, which in moderate amounts can make a valuable contribution to intakes of protein, long-chain fatty acids, B vitamins, vitamin D, iron and zinc. Trimming of all visible fat on meat and removal of skin from poultry should be encouraged, both at retail level and in the home. Selection of lower fat meat products is advisable e.g. lean bacon and lower fat sausages.

3. Meat is an excellent source of haem iron. This form of iron is more easily absorbed than the non-haem iron found in vegetables and cereals.

   Iron deficiency anaemia is the most commonly reported nutritional deficiency in early childhood, so at this age, care must be taken to provide adequate dietary iron. Elimination of meat from the diet, or its severe restriction, may result in a poorer iron status.

   People who are vegetarian, who wish to boost their iron intake, should include foods such as pulses, nuts, fortified breakfast cereals and dark green leafy vegetables, e.g. spinach, in the diet. Food and drink containing vitamin C, e.g. citrus fruits or juice, soft fruits, green vegetables or peppers, can help improve the absorption of iron from these sources when eaten at the same time.

4. Vegetarians have been found to be at reduced risk of coronary heart disease (CHD). This may be owing to the fact that vegetarians tend to be more health conscious. CHD is a complex disease and it is inappropriate to blame any single food for its causation.

5. There is some evidence that high intakes of red and processed meat are associated with colo-rectal cancer. This may however be owing to confounding factors, which are difficult to disentangle, e.g. low fruit and vegetable consumption. The BNF supports the recommendations given in the recent COMA Report (Department of Health 1998)

Lean meat is a nutritious food, which in moderate amounts can make a valuable contribution to intakes of protein, long-chain fatty acids, B vitamins, vitamin D, iron and zinc

that intakes of red meat should be moderate (90g cooked meat per day) and part of an overall balanced and varied diet, which also contains at least five portions of fruit and vegetables a day.

6. Meat should be stored properly in the home, in a fridge at 0-4°C or freezer at −18°C. During preparation, raw and cooked meats should always be kept separate. Frozen meat should be defrosted thoroughly before cooking and should always be cooked or reheated until the temperature reaches at least 70°C (food thermometers can be used to check the temperature). Meat should not be re-frozen. Meat should not be reheated more than once.

Reference

Department of Health (1998). Report on Health and Social Subjects No 48. *Nutritional Aspects of the Development of Cancer*. Committee on Medical Aspects of Food Policy. London: The Stationery Office.

• The above information is an extract from the British Nutrition Foundation's web site which can be found at www.nutrition.org.uk

Vegetarian nutrition

Information from Animal Aid

Some people going vegetarian worry about getting enough protein, calcium, B vitamins and other essential nutrients. The best evidence indicates that a balanced non-animal diet is the healthiest there is – for children as well as for adults.

But the promotion of old-fashioned ideas, combined with the mind-bending power of the meat industry, still cause worries. Here we provide a simple guide to some non-animal sources of the main nutrients.

Protein: Tofu and rice; beans/pulses (peas, lentils) and wholegrains (e.g. beans on toast); tahini and pulse (e.g. houmous); soya milk and cereals; beansprouts and wholegrains. Protein needs are automatically met by a balanced, varied diet.

Fibre: Wholegrains, nuts, beans and pulses, wheatgerm, oats, many fruit and vegetables.

Calcium: Some soya milks, nuts, seeds, green leafy vegetables, tofu and dried fruit.

Vitamin A: Carrots, green leafy vegetables, peppers, margarine, dried apricots.

B vitamins: Yeast extract (e.g. Marmite), nuts, wholemeal bread, rice, mushrooms, bananas, sunflower and sesame seeds.

Selenium: Wholegrains, beans and pulses, nuts.

B12: This vitamin is available in many fortified products (certain soya milks, breakfast cereals, yeast extract, margarine, soya mince and other convenience foods).

Zinc: Lentils, sesame and pumpkin seeds, brown rice and other wholegrains, green vegetables.

Vitamin C: Oranges and other citrus

fruits, blackcurrants, broccoli, spinach, cabbage, potatoes.

Vitamin D: Most people obtain all the vitamin D they need from sunlight on their skin. Certain foods are fortified with it as well, like vegetable margarine.

The best evidence indicates that a balanced non-animal diet is the healthiest there is – for children as well as for adults

---

Vitamin E: Vegetable oils, wheatgerm, avocados, hazelnuts, almonds.

Iron: Baked beans, dried fruit, wholegrains (including bread), molasses, pulses, spinach, cabbage and nuts.

Iodine: Green leafy vegetables, seaweeds, kelp.

Essential fatty acids: Vegetable oils (especially soya, corn, sunflower); avocados, margarine (animal-free); nuts, linseed (flax).

– With grateful thanks to the Physicians' Committee For Responsible Medicine, who were a valuable source for much of this additional information.

• The above information is an extract from Animal Aid's web site which can be found at www.animal aid.org.uk

© Animal Aid

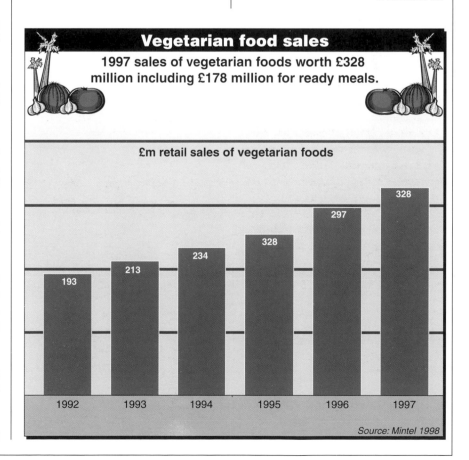

Vegetarian food sales

1997 sales of vegetarian foods worth £328 million including £178 million for ready meals.

£m retail sales of vegetarian foods

1992	1993	1994	1995	1996	1997
193	213	234	328	297	328

Source: Mintel 1998

Meat and fat

Meat matters

Did you know?

- Excess dietary fat is considered one of several risk factors for coronary heart disease.[1]
- Saturated fat tends to raise blood cholesterol.[1]
- Higher levels of blood cholesterol are associated with an increased risk of coronary heart disease.[1]
- About half the fat in lean red meat is unsaturated fat (i.e. monounsaturated and polyunsaturated).
- Meat provides one of the major sources of monounsaturated fat in the British diet (this fat is common in the healthy 'Mediterranean type diet').
- Red meat and meat products contribute less than one-quarter of the total fat intake of all food eaten at home.[2]
- The fat content of lean red meat has fallen by one-third on average over the last 20 years.
- All the essential nutrients in meat are found in the lean parts.

How to reduce fat in the diet

Choose lean cuts of meat and lower-fat products

- Choose lean cubes of beef, lamb or pork for casseroles or kebabs.
- There are ranges of lower-fat versions of popular meat products like sausages, burgers and pâté.

Cut visible fat off meat during preparation or at table

- Trim fat from meat before cooking.
- Cut off any remaining fat on the meat before you eat it.

Check other ingredients of recipe/ meal and swap for low-fat alternatives

- Try a low-fat spread instead of butter or margarine on bread, but whichever you choose, spread it thinly.

Avoid adding extra fat in food preparation

- If you do use any fat when cooking choose oils such as sunflower, corn or olive oil.
- Limit your intakes of oily marinades and salad dressings.

Try these healthier cooking methods such as:

- dry frying, grilling, roasting on a rack or stirfrying
- Skim fat from casseroles and stews before serving.

- Drain and discard fat from the pan before making gravy/ sauce with remaining juices.
- Dab any grilled or fried food before serving

References:

1. British Nutrition Foundation (1997) *Diet and Heart Disease: A round table of factors.* 2nd edition. Ed. Ashwell, M.
2. Ministry of Agriculture, Fisheries and Food (1997) *Household food consumption and expenditure.* National Food Survey, 1996. London: HMSO.

• The above information is an extract from the Meat and Livestock Commission Meat Matters web site which can be found at www.meatmatters.com

© *Meat and Livestock Commission*

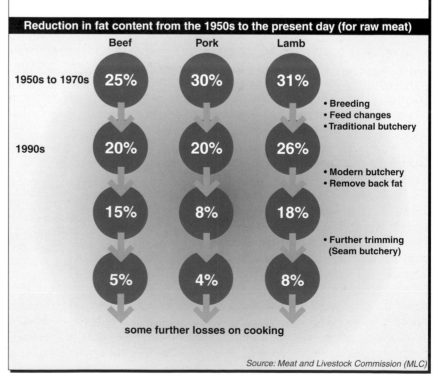

Meat and fat

A healthy diet is a balanced diet which includes a wide variety of foods taken from the four main food groups: bread, other cereals and potatoes; fruit and vegetables; meat, fish and alternatives; milk and dairy foods. Sugars and fats are also an integral part of a balanced diet, but are needed in very small amounts.

Reduction in fat content from the 1950s to the present day (for raw meat)

	Beef	Pork	Lamb	
1950s to 1970s	25%	30%	31%	• Breeding • Feed changes • Traditional butchery
1990s	20%	20%	26%	• Modern butchery • Remove back fat
	15%	8%	18%	• Further trimming (Seam butchery)
	5%	4%	8%	

some further losses on cooking

Source: Meat and Livestock Commission (MLC)

How to be a vegetarian in ten easy steps

Whether it's for health, animal rights, politics or any other reason, you may be considering a vegetarian lifestyle. Here are 10 steps to start you thinking

Read

Research. Explore. Get the facts. Read lots. Knowledge is power.

Think

Think about the animals. Think about your body. Think about the earth. And if you're not tired from all that thinking, consider how your food choices impact the people around you and the world. No need to make any decisions. Just allow yourself time to ponder.

Talk

Talk to vegetarians. Talk to non-vegetarians. Ask questions. Share your thoughts. Join a club. Start a club. Hang out with vegetarians. Then do more thinking.

Set goals

Make a game of it. Bet your friend you can go a whole month without a hamburger or two weeks without eggs and cheese. Setting goals can be serious or fun. Depends on your attitude.

Cook

Learning to cook in a whole new way can be exciting. Take a class. Get books from the store or library. Get *Vegetarian Times* magazine. Try out new recipes on a friend. Do potlucks. Allow yourself to get creative, to play. Have some fun with it. Meatless meals are not only possible, but limitless.

Eat

Make mealtime special. Sit down. Use the good china and cloth napkins. Play nice music (but don't distract yourself with books or TV) before you dig in, and take a moment to be thankful. As you eat, chew carefully, savouring each bite. Slow down. Notice the tastes, sensations. See how it feels to really experience food this way.

Listen

Try to be aware of your body's needs. Sleep when you're tired. Eat when you're hungry. Pay attention to your body – which foods feel good, which don't? Notice how certain foods drain your energy, mood, emotions, concentration and sleep pattern. Respect your body. Learn the connection between what you put in your body and what you get out of it.

Experiment

Try other lifestyle changes. Consider fasting. Look into juicing. Explore macrobiotics or raw food diets. Maybe take up a new sport, or try yoga or jazz dance. Maybe start a journal or learn a new language. Whatever interests you, try it 'as a vegetarian' and see if it feels any different.

Prepare

You may get resistance from friends and family. Be ready for it. (Family dinners can be especially stressful – breaking 'food traditions' is hard on everyone.) Be strong, but not self-righteous. Trust yourself. Prepare, too, for your own self-doubts. Am I getting enough vitamins? Am I doing the right thing? This is normal. Relax. Talk to your friends. Build a support group. Refer back to your books. And if you do 'fall off the wagon', see how you feel, and get back on! Give yourself room to be human, and time to adjust.

Celebrate

Mark the day on your calendar that you stopped eating meat. Celebrate that day! Rejoice in your decision! Have a party. Buy yourself a gift. Treat yourself to a massage. But realise that vegetarianism is an ongoing process, and the 'journey' is more than half the fun!

Whether you see it as a lifestyle, a 'religion', or simply a nutritional choice, vegetarianism is an exciting and beautiful concept. Good luck . . . and enjoy!

The above information is from the web site www.british.meat.co.uk

Vegan FAQs

Information from the Vegan Society

General

What is veganism?
Veganism is a way of living, at least dietary, without the consumption of animal flesh or products.

Why veganism?
Because animals are routinely enslaved and killed for our use and greed.

But why no milk or eggs?
Milk and eggs are still part of the cycle of abuse; cows are impregnated for our unnatural desire for milk, a food that is only ideal for calves. Also many people have an inability to digest lactose in milk (lactose intolerant). Egg production results in the destruction of all the male chicks, the imprisonment of hens in battery farms, and even free range hens are slaughtered as soon as egg laying reduces (1 to 2 years of age).

How did the word VEGAN come about?
The word vegan is a contraction of vegetarian and was coined in the UK in 1944 by the pioneers of the first Vegan Society in the world.

Are there any well-known vegans?
To name but a few:
- Alan Simpson (Member of Parliament)
- Benjamin Zephaniah (poet)
- Alicia Silverstone (actress)
- James (the band all vegan)
- Heather Small (M-People)
- Bryan Adams (singer)
- Judith Shakespeare (champion mountain biker & runner)
- Moby (DJ)
- Paul McGann (actor)
- Robin Gibb (Bee Gees)

Health

Does a vegan diet provide enough protein?
Plant protein is as easily absorbed and as useful to the body as animal protein.

Does a vegan diet provide enough minerals?
A varied and balanced vegan diet provides all the minerals you need.

Does a vegan diet provide enough vitamins?
Again, a varied and balanced vegan diet with fruit, vegetables, grains, nuts and seeds gives all the vitamins but you can take a supplement such as FSCs or Seven Seas they do one suitable for vegans.

Becoming vegan

How can I make the switch?
By gradually cutting out all animal ingredients and replacing them with vegan alternatives e.g. soya milk for cow's milk, vegan cheese etc.

Are there any pitfalls I should watch out for?
There should be no worries with a varied diet providing sufficient calories but, the evidence on whether vegans can obtain a sufficient supply of B12 without supplements is inconclusive, so the Vegan Society recommends that new vegans eat some foods fortified with B12 e.g. soya milk or yeast extract.

Social

Concerned as a parent?
There are various support networks to help vegan families e.g. Leslie Doves. Also the vegan families list and a comprehensive range of factsheets such as pregnancy are available on the web site or directly from the Vegan Society office.

• The above information is an extract from the Vegan Society's web site which can be found at www.vegansociety.com Alternatively, see page 41 for their address details.

© The Vegan Society

Teen vegans

Information from the Vegan Society

Aged between 13 and 19 years of age? Want to be a vegan? You've come to the right place.

There is very little knowledge available on the general eating habits of British teenagers. However, surveys suggest that fat and sugar levels are higher than recommended and that the starch and fibre intake is too low.

The vegan diet is nearer to government health recommendations than any other dietary group in the UK. So, providing teenagers follow the guidelines, transition to a vegan diet should be trouble-free.

Teenagers who follow a vegan diet have the same nutritional needs as any other teenager! Nutritional requirements are high between the ages of 13 and 19 years and it is generally recommended that they eat a wide variety of wholefoods or unrefined foods including fresh fruit and vegetables, bread, pasta, oats and other grains, nuts, seeds and pulses. Care must be taken to ensure protein, calcium, iron and B12 levels are maintained. In other words teenagers, along with the rest of the population, shouldn't live on coke, chips and chocolate!

Teenagers or anyone else thinking of becoming vegan shouldn't think they have to weigh everything before they eat or read nutrition charts before every meal. Once a good understanding of nutrition is grasped, it is recommended to chill out and enjoy!

Famous vegans
- Heather Small – M People
- Moby
- Wendy Turner – *Absolutely Animals*, *Pet Rescue*
- Woody Harrelson – *Natural Born Killers*, *The People Versus Larry Flynt*

'I'm the only vegan in the family'
If you are the only vegan in your family it's not the end of the world.

There are many common foods that everyone can share so you won't feel a nerd. For example most people eat bread, pasta, baked beans, peas, rice, fruit, vegetables, breakfast cereals, biscuits, peanuts, peanut butter, jam, noodles, soup, vegetable curries, Marmite, porridge, etc.

You will also be pleased to know that there are a wide variety of foods that can be used as an alternative to meat and dairy products e.g. soya milk, ice cream, margarine and cream, veggie sausages, sausage rolls and pies. You can even buy vegan chocolate!

There are also many cookery books around now that will give you ideas for meals. The recipes are usually easy to follow and the ingredients can be found in most shops.

Family meal
Make your family a vegan meal once a week to show them you mean business. They will be impressed with your initiative and enjoy the meal too!

Quick nutrition guide
Aim to eat a varied wholefood diet and choose foods from the following food groups on a daily basis:

Cereals
Barley, rice, wheat (bread, pasta), oats, shredded wheat, millet, corn, bulgur, cous cous

Pulses
Beans, peas, lentils (cooked or sprouted)

Nuts and Seeds
All types of nuts, nut butters (peanut butter, cashew nut butter, etc.), pumpkin, sunflower and sesame seeds and tahini (sesame seed spread). Also, sprouted seeds such as alfalfa and mustard

Vegetables (cooked and/or raw)
Deep yellow and dark green leafy vegetables including carrots, green peppers, broccoli, spinach, endive and kale. Other vegetables include bean sprouts, potatoes, tomatoes, lettuce, cabbage, sweetcorn, celery, onions, cucumbers, beetroot, marrows, courgettes and cauliflower

Fruits (fresh, dried and tinned)
Bananas, oranges, tangerines, grapefruit, apples, mangoes, cherries, grapes, apricots, pear, paw paws, kiwis, berries, currants, lemons and plums.

Some vegan sources of key nutrients
Protein
Whole grains (e.g. whole wheat flour and bread, brown rice), nuts (e.g. hazels, cashews, brazils, almonds, cob nuts), seeds (sunflower, sesame, pumpkin), pulses (e.g. peas, beans, lentils), soya flour, soya milk, tofu.

Carbohydrate
Whole grains (e.g. wheat, oats, barley, rice), whole wheat bread, pasta and other flour products, lentils, beans, potatoes, dried and fresh fruit.

Fats

Nuts and seeds, nut and seed oils, vegan margarine, avocados. Two polyunsaturated fatty acids not made by the body are the essential fatty acids linoleic acid (omega 6 group) and alpha linolenic acid (omega 3 group). Good sources of these fatty acids include:

Linoleic acid – safflower, sunflower, corn, evening primrose and soya oils
Alpha-linolenic acid – linseed, pumpkin seed, walnut, soya and rapeseed oils

Vitamins

A – Carrots, spinach, pumpkins, tomatoes, dark green leafy vegetables, vegan margarines

B – Nuts, whole grains, oats, muesli, pulses, yeast extract (e.g. Marmite), leafy green vegetables, potatoes, mushrooms and dried fruit

B12 – Fortified yeast extracts (e.g. Marmite) and soya milks (e.g. Plamil), vegan margarines, packeted 'veggie burger' mixes, some cereals (e.g.Kellogg's Fruit & Fibre, Frosties, Common Sense Oat Bran Flakes). Possibly: fermented foods (e.g. tamari, iso and tempeh), sea vegetables (e.g. hijiki, wakame and spirulina)

C – Citrus fruits (e.g. oranges, lemons, grapefruit), red and blackcurrants, berries, green vegetables and potatoes

D – Sunlight, some soya milks (e.g. Plamil) and vegan margarines

E – Nuts, seeds, whole grains and flours, vegetable oils

Folate – Wheatgerm, raw or lightly-cooked green leafy vegetables (e.g. watercress, broccoli, spinach), yeast, yeast extracts, nuts, peas, runner beans, oranges, dates, avocados, whole grains.

Minerals

Calcium – Molasses, seeds, nuts, carob, pulses, miso (fermented soya bean curd), parsley, figs (dried), sea vegetables, grains, fortified soya milk (several varieties are fortified with calcium)

Nutrition or know your onions!

Information from the Vegan Society

This information is for those of you who wish to know more about nutrition. Further information can be obtained from the book *Vegan Nutrition* by Gill Langley MA, PhD, MIBiol.

Energy
You must make sure you eat enough each day to get plenty of energy. Don't skip meals, don't go hungry and don't fill up with lots of fizzy, sugary drinks and sweets!

You can get energy from all foods but those high in carbohydrates (bread, pasta, potatoes, dried fruit, fruit juice) and fat (vegetable oils, margarine, nuts and seeds) are especially good.

Fat should not contribute more than 35% of the total energy intake of adults and older children.

Estimated average requirements for energy in calories (kcal) / day
- 4-14 yrs (boys) 1715-2220
- 4-14 yrs (girls) 1545-1845
- 15-18 yrs (boys) 2755
- 15-18 yrs (girls) 2110
- 19+ yrs (boys) 2550-2100
- 19+ yrs (girls) 1940-1810

The calorie content of processed foods is listed on the packaging. Foods high in sugar and fat are high in calories.

• The above information is an extract from the Vegan Society's web site which can be found at www.vegansociety.com

© The Vegan Society

Iron – Seeds, nuts, pulses, miso, grains, dried fruit, molasses, sea vegetables, parsley, green leafy vegetables, using cast-iron cookware

Zinc – Wheatgerm, whole grains, nuts, pulses, tofu, soya protein, miso, peas, parsley, bean sprouts

Vegan drinks

Such as tea and coffee (with soya milk of course!), herbal tea, cocoa, fruit juice, mineral water, tap water(!), soft drinks, coffee substitutes such as Barleycup or Caro and soya milk shakes (chocolate, strawberry and vanilla flavours available or make your own!).

A lot of people like Provamel soya milk in their tea or coffee. You can buy a calcium-enriched version (blue carton) for extra calcium or an organic sugar-free version (red carton). For added calcium, vitamin B12 and vitamin D (as well as lots of other good-type nutrients) choose Plamil soya milk. If you don't like the taste of soya milk (I can't believe this!) try disguising the taste by using it in muesli, porridge, custard and rice puddings. You can cook soya milk just like dairy milk so it's a good way of getting extra helpings of calcium, vitamin D and B12. There are lots of different soya milks around – try them all until you find one you like!

Is it going to be expensive?

Vegan foods don't have to be expensive. In fact, if you buy mostly unprocessed foods it will be a lot cheaper. If, however, you want lots of processed foods like sausage rolls and soya cheeses, be prepared to pay.

• The above information is an extract from the Vegan Society's web site which can be found at www.vegansociety.com

© The Vegan Society

Eating for life

Information from PETA Europe Ltd (People for the Ethical Treatment of Animals)

Some people ignore dietary advice to cut back on or cut out animal products, perhaps hoping that a 'magic pill' will come along that will make their illnesses go away. Common sense tells us that prevention is the best medicine. More and more people are finding wonderful ways to tempt their taste buds without tempting fate.

Eliminating animal foods from your diet reduces the risk of some of our biggest killers. According to Dr T. Colin Campbell, nutritional researcher at Cornell University and director of the largest epidemiological study in history, 'The vast majority of all cancers, cardiovascular diseases and other forms of degenerative illness can be prevented simply by adopting a plant-based diet.' Heart disease, cancer, strokes, diabetes, osteoporosis, obesity and other diseases have all been linked to meat and dairy consumption.

It's never too late to change your habits for the better. Changing your diet isn't nearly as inconvenient as enduring a heart bypass operation, suffering paralysis from a stroke or facing chemotherapy and radiation treatments for cancer! Going vegetarian is the single best thing you can do for your health.

- Vegetarianism is an automatic cholesterol-cutter. Dietary cholesterol, which causes heart disease, is found only in animal products.
- A British male meat-eater has a 50 per cent chance of dying of a heart attack, compared to virtually no chance for a pure vegetarian.
- The incidence of high blood pressure is generally greater among meat-eaters than among vegetarians, and cancers of the breast, colon and prostate are more common among people on a high-meat, high-fat, low-fibre diet.
- Meat, dairy products and eggs are completely devoid of fibre and

complex carbohydrates, the nutrients that we're supposed to be consuming more of, and are laden with saturated fat and cholesterol, which make us fat and lethargic in the short term and lead to clogged arteries and heart attacks in the long term.

Q & A: 'What do you think of meat-based diets like the Atkins diet?'
I call them 'the make yourself sick diets' because they cause the body to go into ketosis – a state that occurs when we are seriously ill. I also use that designation because the very foods recommended – meat, chicken,

---

A British male meat-eater has a 50 per cent chance of dying of a heart attack, compared to virtually no chance for a pure vegetarian

---

bacon, eggs, and cheeses – are the foods the Heart Association and the Cancer Society say cause our most dreaded diseases . . . There is only one way to fully satisfy your appetite with delicious foods and stay trim and healthy for a lifetime – that's a low-fat vegetarian diet with fruits and vegetables and a bit of exercise.

Ask the experts: Dr John McDougall, medical director of the McDougall programme

'There's no reason to drink cow's milk at any time in your life. It was designed for calves, not humans, and we should all stop drinking it today.'
Dr Frank A. Oski, former director of pediatrics, Johns Hopkins University

What about protein?
In Western countries, our problem is too much protein, not too little. Most Americans get at least twice as much protein as they need. Almost everything contains protein; unless you eat nothing but junk food, it's almost impossible to eat as many calories as you need for good health without getting enough protein. Healthy sources include whole-wheat bread, oatmeal, beans, pea-

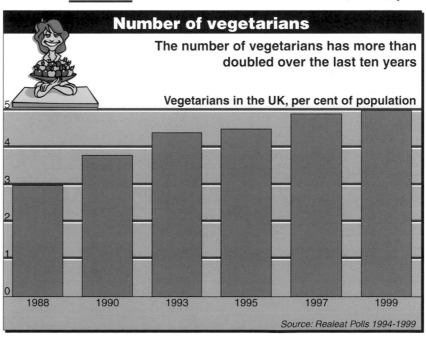

Number of vegetarians

The number of vegetarians has more than doubled over the last ten years

Vegetarians in the UK, per cent of population

Source: Realeat Polls 1994-1999

Milk and eggs	Cholesterol	Calories	Fat	Saturated fat
Milk	34	159	8 grams	4.9 grams
Eggs	274	79	5.6 grams	1.7 grams

nuts, peas, nuts, mushrooms and broccoli.

By contrast, too much protein, especially animal protein, can cause people to excrete calcium through their urine and increase their risk of osteoporosis. Too much protein can also strain the kidneys, leading to kidney disease.

Vegans do not need to combine foods at each meal to get 'complete protein'. All grains, legumes, vegetables, nuts and seeds provide all the essential amino acids.

The average vegetarian lives six years longer than the average meat-eater.

What's wrong with milk and eggs?

No species naturally drinks milk beyond infancy, and no species would naturally drink the milk of a different species. Cow's milk is designed for baby cows, who have four stomachs, double their weight in 47 days and weigh 800 pounds within a year.

For humans, milk has been linked to heart disease, some types of cancer, diabetes and even osteoporosis, the very disease that the dairy industry claims it is supposed to prevent! The high animal-protein content of milk actually causes calcium to be leached from the body. Industrialised Western nations, which are the biggest consumers of milk, have the highest rates of osteoporosis, while regions of the world where dairy products are practically unheard of, such as China and Japan, are virtually osteoporosis-free.

Milk is also loaded with fat and cholesterol and contains an ever-increasing variety of pesticides and antibiotics that are fed to cows. You can get all the calcium you need from the plant world – tofu, broccoli, figs, beans, grain and calcium-fortified orange juice are all good sources.

Serving up just one egg for breakfast each morning can raise your cholesterol level by as much as 10 points! The human body makes all the cholesterol it needs, and when extra cholesterol is eaten, only 100 mg per day can be eliminated – the rest begins clogging the arteries. Women who eat eggs daily triple their risk of breast cancer. Eggs are a primary source of salmonella, which in 1991, sickened 300,000 and caused about 100 deaths in the UK.

'Nothing will benefit human health and increase chances for survival of life on Earth as much as the evolution to a vegetarian diet.'
Albert Einstein

Vegans do not need to combine foods at each meal to get 'complete protein'. All grains, legumes, vegetables, nuts and seeds provide all the essential amino acids

---

'Vegetarians have the best diet. They have the lowest rates of coronary disease of any group in the country . . . they have a fraction of our heart attack rate, and they have only 40 per cent of our cancer rate. On the average, they out live other people by about six years now.'
William Castelli, MD, director, Framingham Heart Study, the longest-running epidemiological study in medical history

Q & A: 'Isn't fish a health food?'
Anyone who eats fish for 'health' reasons should think again: the flesh of fish can accumulate toxins up to 9 million times as concentrated as those in the waters that they live in, and the flesh of some sea animals, like shrimps and scallops, contains more cholesterol than beef. Fish on farms are also fed antibiotics that are passed along to humans, impairing the immune system. And according to the Centers for Disease Control and Prevention, 325,000 people get sick and some die every year in the US from eating contaminated fish and other sea animals.
Ask the experts:
Dr Neal Barnard, author of *Foods That Fight Pain*

• The above information is an extract from PETA Europe Ltd (People for the Ethical Treatment of Animals) web site which can be found at www.petaeurope.com
© PETA Europe Ltd (People for the Ethical Treatment of Animals)

Vegetarians

Seven per cent of the UK adult population is currently vegetarian, among 15-24-year-olds the figure rises to 12 per cent.

Already vegetarian 7%

Could imagine becoming vegetarian 11%

Eating less meat nowadays 41%

Source: NOP Poll for Seven Seas and The Vegetarian Society

Farmers condemn anti-milk campaign aimed at children

A publicity campaign by an American-based vegetarian pressure group intended to persuade primary school children in Britain to stop drinking milk was attacked as irresponsible by farmers and dairy industry leaders yesterday.

The national campaign features 'Milk Sucker' cartoon characters including Spotty Sue, Chubby Charlie, Windy Wendy and Phlegmy Phil on cards which will be distributed to children outside schools. It is due to start in Exeter next week. Slogans on the reverse of the cards warn children that milk is harmful to human health and can make them fat.

The campaign links milk to heart disease, cancer, strokes and osteoporosis – a condition it is supposed to help. Announcing its campaign yesterday, People for the Ethical Treatment of Animals (Peta) admitted the cards were 'eye-catching and stomach-churning' but it justified them as part of its overall campaign to prevent the 'abuse' of cows on intensive dairy farms.

Peta, which is based in Norfolk, Virginia, and claims to have 700,000 members worldwide, including 50,000 in Britain, said: 'On modern mechanised dairy farms cows are treated like nothing more than milk machines – constantly artificially impregnated and genetically manipulated to produce unnaturally large quantities of milk.'

The National Dairy Council, which is currently running a £9 million 'The White Stuff' sales drive, said last night that the Peta campaign was 'totally irresponsible'. Sales of liquid milk have been falling steadily in recent years.

It claimed that the nutritional benefits of drinking milk had been scientifically proved and added: 'While we acknowledge that some people may be emotionally opposed to animal farming on ethical grounds, there is no justification for making

inaccurate and unscientific claims about the health implications of consuming dairy products.'

The National Farmers' Union of England and Wales said: 'This campaign is a scandalous attempt to terrify schoolchildren.' Terrig Morgan, chairman of the NFU's milk and dairy products committee, said: 'The fact that Peta is resorting to emotive tactics on schoolchildren shows that it has lost the logical argument. The campaign is not only inaccurate and misleading, it is downright irresponsible.'

It was 'absolutely ridiculous', he said, to make children believe they would get fat by drinking milk. 'It is against all dietary advice and could be dangerous to children's health.' He added: 'The list of inaccuracies is

> ## The campaign links milk to heart disease, cancer, strokes and osteoporosis – a condition it is supposed to help

endless. For example, it is widely known that there is no evidence that spots are connected to diet. A study published just last week by the University of Bristol showed that drinking milk is good for you – the risk of heart disease, cancer and strokes was lower than for people who drank little milk.'

In Wales, Hugh Richards, president of NFU Cymru, said: 'Dairy farmers across Wales who have the utmost care for their animals are outraged that an organisation peddling such lies intends to influence schoolchildren.

'I have written today to the Welsh Local Government Association and the chief executives of every local authority in Wales asking them to ensure that this material is not distributed in schools in Wales.'

Toni Vernelli, a spokesman for Peta, dismissed the complaints. She said: 'Children would spit out their milk if they knew how cows and calves are treated on intensive dairy farms. Schoolchildren only get one side of the story.'

• By David Brown, Agriculture Editor

The Dairy Council

The Dairy Council condemns pressure group's tactics

The American pressure group PETA has launched a 'Dump Dairy' campaign aimed at primary schoolchildren.

The Dairy Council believes it is totally irresponsible to discourage children from drinking milk, and potentially jeopardise their nutrition status, on the basis of unscientific and misleading arguments. The Food Standards Agency has, today, taken a similar view.

Jill Eisberg, Head of Communications at the Dairy Council, says:

'A large body of scientific evidence supports the nutritional benefits of milk. Milk is one of the most nutritionally complete foods and provides essential nutrients, particularly B vitamins and minerals.

'Young children in particular rely on cows' milk to provide them with a significant proportion of essential nutrients. A 200ml glass of milk provides a 6-year-old with over half his or her daily requirement of calcium, as well as many other vitamins and minerals.

'While we acknowledge that some people may be emotionally opposed to animal farming on ethical grounds, this is no justification for making inaccurate and unscientific claims about the health implications of consuming dairy products.

'Eliminating highly nutritious foods such as milk and dairy products from the diet may lead to long-term health problems, and should not be done without good reason.'

Notes

Animal welfare

- It is in the dairy farmer's own interest to ensure that his herds are healthy and unstressed. Contented cows produce more milk, and this increased productivity results in better value for the consumer and a better financial return for the farmer.
- The UK dairy industry takes pride in keeping up to date with advances in animal care, health and welfare.

Milk and obesity

- There is no evidence that consuming milk and dairy products per se makes you fat. It is a myth that milk is high in fat. Whole milk contains only 4% fat, semi-skimmed milk less than 2% and skimmed milk is virtually fat free.

Milk and mucus

- There is no scientific evidence to support the belief that milk and dairy products increase mucus production.

Lactose intolerance

- Only around 2% of the population are lactose intolerant and it is not common in children. Research shows that most people with lactose intolerance can drink a 120ml glass of milk on an empty stomach, and consume hard cheese (which is virtually lactose-free) and yogurts, without experiencing wind or other symptoms.

Osteoporosis

- Getting enough calcium for strong bones during the first two decades of life is particularly important, as we cannot make up for any shortfall later on. Dairy products are the best source of easily absorbed calcium and research suggests they may help protect against osteoporosis.

Acne

- There is no evidence that drinking milk causes spots. In fact, dermatologists agree that diet in general has very little effect on skin health, except in very rare cases. Acne is caused by the oil glands in the skin producing too much oil. This is caused by hormone changes, not diet.

Heart disease

- There is no scientific evidence to support the claim that drinking milk and eating dairy products per se, which provide some saturated fat, increases the risk of heart disease. In fact, a study from Bristol University, published last week, shows that men who consumed over a third of a pint of whole milk every day over 25 years reduced their risk of heart disease by 8%.

Stroke

- Researchers have demonstrated that high intakes of low-fat dairy foods and fruit and vegetables significantly lower blood pressure, a significant risk factor for stroke.

Cancer

- To date, the scientific evidence for a link between dairy products and cancer is contradictory. Emerging research actually suggests that components of milk fat (CLA, sphingomyelin and butyric acid) have anti-cancer properties. A high calcium intake from dairy products has also been related to a lower risk of colon cancer.

• The above information is an extract from the Dairy Council's web site which can be found at www.milk.co.uk

Vegetarians offered discount cover

A UK company has launched a life insurance scheme to reward vegetarians for their lifestyle choice.

The insurance is being offered by Animal Friends Insurance (AFI), which came up with the idea after statistics showed that vegetarians were less likely to suffer from chronic illness than meat eaters.

The policy, which is underwritten by Liverpool Victoria Life Company, gives vegetarians a 25% discount for the first year, and any profits made from the sale are donated to animal welfare groups.

The 25% reduction is a 12-month discount and works by rebating commission paid to AFI. Elaine Fairfax, who founded AFI with her husband Chris, said: 'Epidemiological evidence indicates that vegetarians suffer less from chronic disease, but the insurance industry has not yet recognised this.'

She said the industry had been very quick to put up premiums because of the negative effects of smoking, but it had not yet cut premiums to reflect the positive effects of being a vegetarian.

Research carried out by the Oxford Vegetarian Society found that vegetarians are 30% less likely to develop heart disease and 39% less likely to develop cancer than meat eaters.

In order to qualify for the insurance, applicants will have to follow the same procedure that smokers and non-smokers do when applying for insurance. They will have to sign a legal declaration stating that they do follow a vegetarian lifestyle. Although this could lead to carnivores being flexible with the truth, Mr Fairfax doesn't think this will be a problem.

'The insurance industry knows that a small percentage of people will lie on their application forms and it will adjust premiums accordingly,' he said. 'In addition to

this, if someone does die of a heart attack, for example, their cholesterol levels will show whether they were meat eaters, and if this is the case their insurance claim will be void.'

Mr Fairfax also added that there were 'definite indications' that insurance discounts for vegetarians could become more widespread. He said a number of insurers had expressed an interest in looking more closely at the data that indicate that vegetarians are less likely to develop chronic illnesses.

'Epidemiological evidence indicates that vegetarians suffer less from chronic disease, but the insurance industry has not yet recognised this'

The insurance, which is aimed at the UK's four million vegetarians, has been launched in association with the Vegetarian Society in time for National Vegetarian Week, which starts on Monday.

AFI also sells motor, travel, pet, commercial and critical illness insurance, and all profits made by the group are donated to charities such as the Born Free Foundation, Compassion in World Farming, and the Vegetarian Society.

However, despite the apparent appeal of the deal to vegetarians, one discount broker is already saying that customers could do better elsewhere.

'AFI customers only get their discount for the first year's cover,' says John Beale, of discount broker Torquil Clark. 'But a quick check on the rates, discounts and cash-backs on offer show that vegetarians, omnivores and carnivores could do better with us.'

Mr Beale said the customer could then decide if they wanted to give some or all of this saved cash to charity. He added that this donation could also be boosted by giving under one of the government's tax beneficial charity-giving schemes.

© *Guardian Newspapers Limited 2001*

Vegetarians and heart disease

Information from the Coronary Prevention Group

Adopting a vegetarian diet is becoming an increasingly popular decision in the UK: it is estimated that around 7% of adults are vegetarian, 4 million people! The numbers avoiding red meat are even higher. People become vegetarian for many reasons including ethics, health, religion and economics. But what exactly is a vegetarian diet? Strictly speaking a vegetarian eats no fish, shellfish, poultry, game or meat but will normally eat eggs and dairy products. A vegan, on the other hand, will eat no animal products at all including eggs, milk or honey. It is perfectly feasible, whatever your age, to obtain all the energy, protein and nutrients you need with or without eating meat – it's your choice.

Vegetarian diets and heart disease

There is good evidence that vegetarians are less likely than non-vegetarians to die from coronary heart disease. Studies have found that mortality from heart disease is 24% lower in vegetarians of all ages. This implies that if everyone were to have a vegetarian diet, then 40,000 deaths from heart disease could be prevented every year. The younger you are, however, the more a vegetarian diet seems to protect you: heart disease mortality is 45% lower in vegetarians under 65 years of age! The protective effect of a vegetarian diet only seems to be apparent if a person has been vegetarian for at least 5 years though.

If you enjoy the occasional chicken wing or sausage sandwich though there's no need to despair. It has been found that people who eat meat occasionally (less than once a week) and people who eat fish also have significantly lower levels of mortality from coronary heart disease than regular meat eaters.

So what is it about vegetarians that makes them so healthy? It is important to remember that people who are vegetarian may also be more conscious about other aspects of their health and lifestyle. They are often found to smoke and drink less, and exercise more than non-vegetarians. Vegetarians tend to be thinner than meat eaters on average and consequently are less likely to be obese – a major risk factor for coronary heart disease. Vegetarians also tend to have lower levels of blood cholesterol, another important risk factor.

Studies of vegetarians' diets have found that they don't necessarily eat fewer calories than meat eaters but their calories come from different sources. They tend to eat more starchy carbohydrate (bread, pasta, rice etc.) and more fibre. They may eat less saturated fat (although switching meat for cheese won't help reduce saturated fat intakes!) and more polyunsaturated fat.

Other parts of the diet which may be beneficial include anti-oxidant vitamins and flavonoids.

A healthy vegetarian diet

A diet of chips and chocolate is a still a vegetarian diet; it is important to remember that the absence of meat and fish doesn't automatically bestow everlasting life upon you! Whether or not you choose to include small amounts of meat in your diet, the characteristics of a good vegetarian diet could benefit everyone. These include plenty of fruits and vegetables (frozen, tinned, dried or fresh), wholegrain starchy foods such as pastas, wholemeal bread and rice, and pulses (peas and beans).

• The above information is an extract from the Coronary Prevention Group's web site which can be found at www.healthnet.org.uk

© Healthnet – 1995/2000

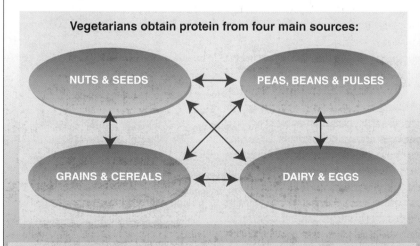

Protein

Girls aged 15-18 years need around 45g of protein a day (more, if very active or lactating) and boys aged 15-18 need about 55g (more if very active). Too much protein may aggravate poor or failing kidney function.

Vegetarians obtain protein from four main sources:

NUTS & SEEDS ↔ PEAS, BEANS & PULSES

GRAINS & CEREALS ↔ DAIRY & EGGS

The humble soya bean is an excellent source of vegetarian protein and is found in veggie bacon, tofu, pot noodles, sausages and sauces! It can be made into milk and other dairy substitutes for vegans. It is also consumed widely by omnivores as soya is found (as a bulking agent) in 70% of processed foods.

Source: The Vegetarian Society

Cheat meat

Ten years ago, cardboard-like soya sausages were as good as it got. Today we have fake bacon, pork-free pork pies, liverless pate, chickenless tikka, fishless fishcakes . . . Emma Brockes on the next generation of vegetarian food

The chef is aiming a cautious spatula at the fry-up under the grill. It looks like an ordinary breakfast: bacon blistering, sausage blooming liver spots, two glum burgers sweating in the heat. 'It'll need a bit of oil,' says Adam Eastwood, who jack-knifes across the kitchen. 'That sausage is still too anaemic.' When he unveils the finished meal, the staff of the Manchester restaurant crane their necks to stare at it.

The bacon is made from fermented soya beans, raw cane sugar and something called locust bean gum. The frankfurters are oat flakes, apples, breadcrumbs and spices. The burgers are brown rice and tofu. They are the new generation of meat substitutes, the heirs to those rehydrated soya sausages that, 10 years ago, were the vegetarian's only recourse to the pleasures of the carnivore. In the past couple of years the cheating meat market has exploded from a few mean-looking burgers and some chewy Quorn, to vegetarian caviar and roast 'turkey'.

Analogue meat products and veggie ready meals are now the biggest sellers in the vegetarian food market. There is fake ham, fake beef and fake chicken roll, fishless fishcake and porkless pork pie, the chickenless tikka and the liverless pate. Scrolling down the product range is like reading an ingredients list from one of those heartbreaking wartime cookbooks, in which ration-stricken housewives were instructed on how to make roast duck out of carrots. The question is, why, in a time of plenty, would anyone want to return to it?

There are more than three million vegetarians in the UK, equivalent to 5.4% of population, and thousands more of what the Vegetarian Society calls 'vegetarian-appreciators', those who buy veggie

food as they would Chinese or Indian. Earlier this year, a report published by Mintel market research put the value of the vegetarian food market for 2000 at £428m, £143m of which went on meat substitutes. The latter is double the figure for 1995 and the veggie market's most rapid area of growth. This is in spite of the fact that the very idea of fake meat is repulsive to many vegetarians and thoroughly ridiculed by meat-eaters. What an advert for the human body's irrepressible craving for meat is the porkless pork pie!

In the past couple of years the cheating meat market has exploded from a few mean-looking burgers and some chewy Quorn, to vegetarian caviar and roast 'turkey'

From the outset, therefore, the concept of meat substitutes has divided vegetarians into two camps: those who have abandoned meat for ethical reasons but still wet dream about bacon sandwiches, and those who simply find meat disgusting.

'For some vegetarians the taste, texture and smell of meat is exactly what they seek to avoid,' says Samantha Calvert of the Vegetarian Society. 'They've broken away from the meat-eating world and they can't understand why manufacturers would think they wanted to eat those products. These are the ones who occasionally take the moral high ground and dictate that other vegetarians should be the same as them.'

Jeremy King is the manager of Redwood Foods, the company behind cheatin' roast turkey, vegetarian rashers and a range of cold 'meat' slices. 'There are plenty of vegetarians who like bacon but don't want the pig to go,' he says. 'In the old days, a vegetarian burger used to be a bit of peas and veg stuck together. The technology has advanced so much that we are delivering meat substitutes with real texture and flavouring.' Their advantage over traditional veggie food, he says, is one of variety: the options available to a vegetarian child who takes a packed lunch to school are instantly multiplied by cheating lunchmeats.

It all depends of course on what this stuff tastes like. In terms of smell, the vegetarian fry-up cooked by volunteer chef Adam Eastwood is spot on. The bacon smells bacony, although it is the colour of corned beef or salami. When you break it in two, it offers some authentic, piggy resistance and frays at the tear line. There is a bacon-like grain on its surface. The sausages are pasty looking, like one of those white cheese snacks that come in a sheath, and the burgers are too uniform around the edges to be credible. They need those distressed bits of overhang you get in a McDonald's patty to pass. Still, to the untrained eye, the whole package looks pretty good.

Eastwood used to work in the kitchens of Zeneca, a company that pioneered Quorn, and nibbles at the rasher's edges. 'Mmmm,' he says, turning away to swallow. His face contorts. 'It's too salty. It tastes like the flavour you get on smoky bacon crisps. It's like they've taken that flavour and put it on some cardboard. But the sausage looks OK.'

To those meat-eaters who can't pass a field of lambs without triggering a major guilt complex, the main obstacle to becoming a vegetarian has always been the hassle factor. Convenience food is still predominantly aimed at the meat-eating market and the idea of faffing about with vegetable recipes is too much bother. Part of the appeal of the new products is that they can be slammed into a sandwich like a traditional slice of ham, or bunged in the oven with the Christmas turkey.

The party line at the Vegetarian Society is that anything that greases the path to vegetarianism is a good thing. 'When people first become vegetarians it can be easier for them if there is a substitute product that they can put directly into their old meals,' says Samantha Calvert. 'If they're making a lasagne they can just throw in a mince substitute and know exactly where they are.' They don't have to throw out their cookbooks or even modify them. And, as the manufacturers are no doubt aware, the longer they are vegetarians, the more distant the memory of how genuine meat tastes grows.

Animal culls 'turning people into vegetarians'

People have been so traumatised by the distressing images of thousands of animals being slaughtered and dumped in mass graves that they are considering vegetarianism.

The Vegetarian Society said it had been 'inundated' by calls from people across the country who have found the foot-and-mouth outbreak 'the final straw'.

Thousands of people ranging from children to a woman in her 80s had called in the past two months asking for advice about a vegetarian diet, said a society spokeswoman.

'We have been very busy with calls, up 100% in March compared to January's figures from members of the public.

'It is mainly people who have made the decision to become vegetarian on the back of the foot-and-mouth crisis. People have seen the images of animals being killed, thrown around, left dead on farms and put on to fires.

'Other people just have a longer feeling of distrust with meat,' she added.

Some calls were from parents whose children have been so upset by the images that they had asked to stop eating meat. 'We had a call from a woman in her 80s from Jersey who had become a veggie. Having seen and heard all about this she decided she could never eat meat again,' the spokeswoman said.

The society's statement came as members of campaign group Viva! were set to dress in lamb costumes outside one of the country's busiest railway stations and unfold a giant banner saying: 'If killing "healthy" lambs upsets you – don't eat them'.

The group will be urging Londoners at Liverpool Street station to go vegetarian and offer free information to help them make the change. Spokeswoman Juliet Gellatley said: 'People have to ask themselves what it is that upsets them about the killing of lambs. It certainly won't stop when foot-and-mouth does. If they are genuinely disturbed then they should stop eating them.'

The Vegetarian Society said it had been 'inundated' by calls from people across the country who have found the foot-and-mouth outbreak 'the final straw'

Welcome return to pleasures of flesh

Penny Stuttaford readies herself to indulge

This Christmas, for the first time in nine years, I'll be having turkey with all the trimmings – and I can't wait. Since the age of 19, I've tried non-dairy, non-wheat, low-carb, low-fat and even fruit-and-veg-only diets, the one constant being the lack of meat. I was never smug – but there was a certain inner confidence that I would surely be rewarded for not clogging my arteries with animal fats.

I became a staunch vegetarian in 1991, induced by a year of travel that began in India. It was primarily a health issue, which – over time – became a question of morals. This was largely due to the bullying I received from non-vegetarians, relentless in their pursuit of an argument for abstaining from the Sunday roast. I came up with, 'I won't eat what I wouldn't kill', which I was rather pleased with; it seemed to placate them.

During my world tour, I hitch-hiked around Australia with my then boyfriend. We must have been a peculiar sight on those endless roads. I'd come from my meditation classes in Dharamasala, in flowing silk saris, embracing my new vegetarian diet and avoiding the smallest living thing in my path – so as not to incur any karmic debt. He'd been working on a sheep station in New South Wales, hadn't seen a vegetable in weeks and had lived on a diet of lamb, beer and white bread for a month. He'd gained a stone for the one I'd lost. We were diametrically opposed: I should have foreseen the end of our two-year relationship then and there.

Instead, I tested it to the limit by suggesting a trip to Mooloo, a yoga retreat near Brisbane. Nicky and James ran it from an old Queenslander house; they used only biodegradable products, ate nothing but fruit and vegetables and practised yoga every morning from five until 10.

I was affected hugely during my stay by the vitality of 56-year-old Nicky: she exuded health, had a taut, svelte physique, the brightest of eyes and the clearest of skins. We talked at length about nutrition and the merits of her fruit-and-vegetable diet versus one of meat and processed food. I was sold; I now had living proof that man can live on fruit and vegetables alone. For the remainder of the trip, I became a bit puritanical, chiding the boyfriend for eating crisps and preaching to all about my new diet.

I have since settled down and don't have to eat meat at every meal. But I've never felt better and friends say I have a certain 'glow' about me

---

On my return to Britain, I went to university and soon discovered the life of an undergraduate was not conducive to the healthy routine I'd enjoyed on my travels. Friends teased me as I donned a large rucksack twice weekly to stock up with fresh produce from the local market. The smell of rotting fruit lingered wherever I went.

I abandoned academia for acting and, about the same time, I found it was more practical to become what is known in my family as a pescatarian. The fish seemed to agree with me, my energy levels soared and my intake increased to such an extent that I was given the nickname Minke (as in whale). It seemed that my body couldn't get enough – I would think nothing of consuming a large catfood-sized tin of tuna for lunch each day.

And then I came across an article on eating to suit your blood group. As a would-be yogi, I hoped and assumed that I would be blood type AB – the photo showed a slim lentil-eating water guzzler – or at the very least the golfclub-swinging type A representative who 'responds best to vegetarianism'. I rummaged for my blood donor card – and found I was in fact group O, requiring vigorous exercise and for whom 'many meats are good'.

The first crack had appeared in my philosophy. This was confirmed when I went to a nutritionist in Cardiff. She started me off on a diet that included guinea fowl, turkey and lamb.

For my first foray into the world of meat, I gingerly placed two turkey breasts under the grill, smothering them in a creamy sauce and telling myself they were swordfish steaks. In fact, I needn't have bothered. I took to my new diet straight away. I've even gravitated back to an intolerance of those who go without meat; I quickly forgot all my recipes and usually snarl at those coming to dinner who won't eat it.

I have since settled down and don't have to eat meat at every meal. But I've never felt better and friends say I have a certain 'glow' about me – though that could be the Ashtanga yoga.

Animal welfare

Information from the Food and Farming Education Service

Introduction

Humans have kept animals for their meat, milk, wool and hides for many thousands of years. For much of this time the ways in which the animals were kept and treated by their owners changed very little. The animals would be cared for, as well as possible, because they were very valuable to the owner.

In more recent times, particularly in the last 100 years, many changes have taken place in the way these domesticated animals are reared. These changes were in order to meet the demands for food from a rapidly increasing population.

Very intensive animal husbandry systems have been developed to produce a maximum amount of food at a minimum cost. In some of these systems the animals may be denied some of their natural requirements.

As we become more knowledgeable about animal needs (which may be very different from those of humans), the way in which animals are kept will also change to provide a more suitable environment for them to live in. However, it should not automatically be assumed that more extensive systems are always better for the animals.

Any animals kept in the service of man should be protected from unnecessary suffering. Anyone caring for them requires an understanding of their needs.

Legislation

At an international level Britain has led the way in developing the first legislation regarding farm animal welfare with the Careful Treatment of Cattle Act of 1822. This was followed in 1835 by the Cruelty to Animals Act.

Present legislation on the welfare of farm animals is based upon

recommendations contained in a report by a Government technical committee: the Brambell Committee. This committee felt that the laws relating to animal welfare needed improving and their recommendations led directly to the Agriculture (Miscellaneous Provisions) Act, 1968.

Under this Act any person who knowingly causes unnecessary pain or distress to any farm animal is liable to prosecution. Also, the Government can set up Codes of Practice about what treatment of animals is permitted and the State Veterinary Service is allowed entry to farms to inspect stock and give advice on welfare matters.

The Farm Animal Welfare Council, an independent body, advises Government who, in turn, publish Codes of Conduct. These Codes are circulated to all farmers and provide guidance on welfare for each species of animal.

New EU and Government legislation aims to improve the welfare of farm animals.

The welfare needs of animals can be defined by the 'five freedoms' which were set out by the Farm Animal Welfare Council in 1992:

1. Freedom from hunger and thirst – the animals should be able to drink fresh water whenever they need it and they should be fed on a diet which keeps them healthy and strong.
2. Freedom from chronic discomfort – the animals should be kept in a comfortable environment.
3. Freedom from injury and disease – the environment that the animals live in shall be safe for them and not cause them injury.
4. Freedom to express normal behaviour – the animals should be able to move around easily and mix with other animals in their group.
5. Freedom from fear and the avoidance of stress whenever possible – the animals should not be kept in conditions where they are afraid or where they might suffer any unnecessary pain or distress. This also applies when they are in transport, at markets or abattoirs.

Most farming practices have been developed over the years to meet the public's demand for sufficient supplies of food at a relatively low cost. However, some of these practices are now considered by certain people to be inappropriate for the welfare of the animals involved.

Welfare issues

The main farm animal welfare issues in the 1990s are:

Poultry

The majority of laying hens are kept in cages where they have a limited amount of space to move. They may suffer from loss of feathers and foot problems, but are warm, provided with light, food and water and are in groups where fighting and cannibalism does not take place.

Pigs

What type of housing will replace stalls and tethers for breeding sows now that they have been banned by the Government? What are the welfare implications for the increasing number of outdoor pig units?

Transportation

Live animals, particularly sheep, are often transported over very long distances. A code of practice for hauliers requires agreement and implementation across Europe.

Markets and abattoirs

Ensuring that animals are humanely treated as they go through the markets and abattoirs.

Farm buildings

Farm buildings constructed in recent years are usually designed to allow the most efficient farming of livestock at the minimum of cost. Increasingly, their design must meet certain legal requirements. On older farms existing buildings have often been adapted to meet these requirements.

In the future, the design of farm buildings will need to take account of animal welfare more than ever before. The Animal Welfare Codes specify the following requirements:

1. There should be sufficient lighting to allow inspection of animals at all times;
2. There should be no sharp edges or damaged parts of the structure;
3. All structures used for holding stock should be secure and strong;
4. There should be adequate space

Any animals kept in the service of man should be protected from unnecessary suffering

---

for the animals to move around and there should also be dry lying areas;
5. There should be special pens for calving cows and also for any sick or injured animals;
6. The buildings need good ventilation and should be kept clean and free from dust.

Transportation of live animals

All farm animals, at some time during their lives, have to be transported from the farm to markets, agricultural shows, other farms or to the slaughterhouse. It is possible to see lorries full of sheep or cattle which have been specially designed for this purpose. The animals are usually packed closely together but this is to stop them falling over and injuring themselves.

Normally the farmers will take their stock to the nearest livestock market or abattoir, unless the animals are being put into a specialist sale such as those for bulls or rams, held regionally.

Some animals are sold for live export to countries in Europe and further afield. A few of these will be very high quality animals which will be used for breeding purposes.

However, the vast majority of animals exported will be slaughtered for meat when they reach their destination. This is because of the consumer demands in these particular countries where people prefer to have their meat slaughtered locally.

Animals travelling from Scotland, for example, may have to endure very long journeys through countries where the climate may be very much hotter than they are used to. Once in mainland Europe the regulations allow animals to travel for more than 24 hours without a break and there is therefore a need to develop regulations for the whole of Europe so that this is more tightly controlled.

This export market has been affected by the world-wide ban on beef products imposed by the EU in 1996 in response to the BSE crisis. Now far fewer animals are exported than before the crisis.

In 1995 the EU issued a Directive on the transportation of live animals.

The new requirements included:
- A maximum journey time of 8 hours for horses, cattle, pigs, sheep and goats when carried in 'ordinary' haulage floats; on completion of this maximum journey length the animals should be rested for 24 hours. This 8-hour maximum journey time may be extended in vehicles with higher specifications and which provide sufficient feed for the type of animals being transported;
- Direct access to the animals;
- Adequate ventilation which can be adjusted to temperatures, both inside and outside;
- Movable partitions to create separate compartments that are equipped with a connection to water supply during stops;
- Vehicles carrying pigs must carry sufficient water for drinking during the journey.

A new system for selling animals without the need for them to be taken to market is being pioneered in Scotland. It is known as an Electronic Auction System. When a farmer has animals he wishes to sell a fieldsman from the company operating the system comes to the farm. The animals for sale are selected, their details are noted and a price is discussed with the farmer. These details are entered into a computer. Buyers bid for the animals using computer terminals in their offices. Only when the animals have been sold are they removed from the farm, and taken direct to their destinations. This is a much more humane system than taking them to market where they are unloaded, sold, reloaded and further transported.

Auction markets

Nearly every farm animal at some time during its life will be taken to an auction market for sale, either to another farmer or to a dealer for meat.

Livestock markets and fairs have a very long tradition going back to the 9th century and auction markets were first introduced in 1836. Both the owner of the animals and the auctioneers will want the animals to look their best and may prepare them by washing and brushing them. The animal welfare considerations relating to animals at livestock markets include the accommodation, handling methods and facilities for dealing with sick or injured animals.

Welfare at markets has improved greatly over the past few years and there are many legal requirements placed on those running the markets to help to ensure that the animals in their care are treated as well as possible. Welfare Officers, employed by the District Councils, are legally required to be present at markets to enforce the regulations.

Abattoirs

Nearly all farm animals are reared for their meat and when they reach a certain weight they will be taken from the farm to the abattoir to be slaughtered.

During the Second World War meat was rationed and many of the smaller abattoirs closed down. Development after this time concentrated on a small number of abattoirs and this has meant that the enforcement of welfare standards has been made easier.

There are now many more legal requirements which the abattoir owner must meet. In addition to our own strict laws there are also European laws that govern animal welfare. Increasingly fewer abattoir owners are capable of finding the large amounts of money required to make the necessary improvements, particularly in relation to food hygiene. Because of this, in recent years, many have been forced to close down.

At the abattoir the animals will be stunned before being killed. However, both the Jewish and Muslim communities are permitted to kill animals without stunning them first. They are only allowed to eat meat killed in this way as it is part of their religious beliefs.

Go veggie

Information from Viva!

Why go vegetarian?

By changing your diet, you start to change the world. By going vegetarian, you strengthen our collapsing environment and strike a blow for fairness in the developing world. You improve your health and life expectancy. And you no longer play a part in the abuse of billions of animals.

Feed the world
Starvation and famine are not natural calamities. They are mostly man-made – and the meat in your butcher's windows plays a major part.

Livestock farming is extremely wasteful. Land that can support two meat-eating people can feed up to 60 people on plant foods. There are now so many animals that huge quantities of food are imported from the developing world – often the same countries whose children die from starvation. By giving up meat you remove yourself from this cycle of exploitation.

Protect the environment
More than 43 billion farmed animals are killed every year worldwide. Rainforests are felled and whole ecosystems are burned to provide their grazing. Precious water is squandered on growing fodder to feed to them. Their over-grazing is turning one-third of the planet into desert. Fertilisers and pesticides used to grow their fodder are destroying the ozone layer and decimating life.

The world's oceans are collapsing because of overfishing. All sea creatures have been poisoned with deadly chemicals – so you are officially advised to limit how much fish you eat. By not eating fish at all, you help preserve the oceans and your own health.

Improve your health
Vegetarians are healthier and live longer than meat eaters. Simply by changing your diet you reduce your risk of heart disease, high blood pressure, strokes, obesity, cancers and many other diseases. All the world's advisory bodies agree – fresh fruit, vegetables and plant foods protect against disease, animal proteins, fat and cholesterol help cause it. And then, of course, there's BSE, antibiotic-resistant killer bugs, salmonella, E coli, campylobacter... and their favourite home is meat!

End animal suffering
Society boasts of its humanity yet crams restless, strutting hens five to a wire cage no bigger than a microwave oven. It imprisons an intelligent animal like a pig in a metal crate so small she can never turn around and goes mad with the stress. One-day-old dairy calves are taken away from their mothers and shot. Sheep are tricked into lambing in bitter midwinter, resulting in four million deaths from cold each year.

Most meat animals are crammed into factory farms to live their lives standing in filth. Why was it ever allowed to happen and why do so many believe the lies about good welfare? Their best protection is not to eat them.

Animals and the environment

Information from the Vegetarian Society

Vegetarians reduce animal suffering and slaughter
In the UK alone, 800 million animals are slaughtered for food each year.

These animals are as feeling as any household pet and, in many cases, far more intelligent.

Yet they are still forced to live tortuous, short lives; denied access to their young, deprived of basic freedoms, fed on unnatural diets and chemicals, kept in cramped conditions where they frequently develop physical and psychological abnormalities.

Then they're transported from factory farm, to livestock market, then to the horrors of the slaughterhouse.

Some have to endure the long, stressful haul to markets abroad, often in extremes of weather without adequate provisions such as food, water, air and light, to places where conditions are even worse. They are then killed.

A vegetarian diet is better for the environment
Meat and fish production is damaging the Earth beyond repair. Here's how:
- Methane-emitting livestock contribute massively to the 'Greenhouse Effect' and global warming.
- Ammonia from animal waste and agricultural fertilisers contribute to acid rain which kills aquatic and plant life.
- Livestock farming makes inefficient use of limited resources. Millions of people go hungry and thirsty in the developing world while grain and water is squandered on rearing animals to be slaughtered for food in the developed world.
- Millions of hectares of life-sustaining rain forest are destroyed each year to create grazing pasture. This kills off and puts at risk animal species and indigenous human populations.
- Over-fishing of the Earth's oceans has decimated fish populations to the point of near extinction of many species. Dolphins and whales are indiscriminately killed by drift nets while massive amounts of dead fish are thrown back into the sea or used as pig and sheep feed.
- Intensive grazing causes soil erosion and nutrient depletion.

These are just some of the many ways meat and fish production are harming our world. A vegetarian diet makes better use of the world's resources and is a highly effective way of positively contributing to our planet's future. Together we can make the world a better place.

- The above information is an extract from the Vegetarian Society's web site which can be found at www.vegsoc.org

© The Vegetarian Society

Freedom food

The RSPCA's welfare-friendly food labelling scheme.
RSPCA – committed to farm animal welfare

What is the Freedom Food scheme?

Freedom Food Ltd is an independent, non-profit making organisation set up by the RSPCA to improve farm animal welfare in the UK. The Freedom Food label on meat, eggs and dairy products is your assurance that the product has come from animals reared, transported and slaughtered in accordance with welfare standards compiled by the RSPCA.

The RSPCA set up Freedom Food Ltd as a wholly owned subsidiary in July 1994 to help improve the lives of the UK's 860 million farm animals and to provide consumers with a clear welfare choice. Many of the UK's farm animals are still kept in conditions which can result in considerable suffering.

Freedom Food's welfare standards are written by the RSPCA's farm animal specialists in consultation with veterinary surgeons, farm animal experts and producers. The standards are based on the needs of the animals and are written around scientific research and practical farming experience.

Welfare standards have been written for the following species: sheep, chickens, turkeys, laying hens, ducks, beef cattle, dairy cattle and pigs. The standards are regularly reviewed and amended according to the latest research.

Five freedoms

The RSPCA standards are based on five freedoms that all farm animals deserve:
- Freedom from fear and distress
- Freedom from pain, injury and disease
- Freedom from hunger and thirst
- Freedom from discomfort
- Freedom to express normal behaviour

Freedom from fear and distress . . .
All who manage and handle livestock need to understand the basics of

animal behaviour, in order to avoid stress to animals, particularly when they are being moved, loaded or unloaded.

Mixing different social groups, ages and sexes of animals can also be very stressful and even result in injury. Freedom Food requires that this risk is minimised.

Freedom from pain, injury and disease . . .

Animals must be protected from injury and from elements which may cause pain or ill health. Their environment must be well managed to promote good health and they must receive swift veterinary attention whenever necessary. The standards require all farms to have a Veterinary Health Plan.

Freedom from hunger and thirst . . .

Diet must be satisfying, appropriate and safe. Bullying and competition during feeding are minimised by specifying generous feeding and drinking space allowances. The animals must have continuous access to clean, fresh water.

Freedom from discomfort . . .

A clean, dry, comfortable bedded lying area and plenty of space to move around must be provided, as well as shelter to protect animals from the weather. The RSPCA standards stipulate space allowances to ensure that all animals have adequate room to lie down comfortably, groom themselves, and get up and down easily. The environment must take into account the animals' welfare needs and be designed to protect them from physical and thermal discomfort.

Freedom to express normal behaviour . . .

By providing sufficient space, proper facilities and company of the animals' own kind. For example, a laying hen must be able to perch, dust bathe, move around, stretch, and flap her wings, as well as have a safe, comfortable resting area and a separate nest box area in which to lay her eggs. The compulsory provision of bedding for pigs not only means that there is a comfortable lying place, it also enriches the

---

A clean, dry, comfortable bedded lying area and plenty of space to move around must be provided, as well as shelter to protect animals from the weather

---

environment by giving an opportunity for exploration, rooting behaviour and play.

How does the Freedom Food scheme work?

Enquiry from farmer, producer, haulier or abattoir

Freedom Food sends out a copy of the RSPCA welfare standards appropriate to the species with a pre-registration form. This is completed by the interested party and returned to Freedom Food.

Formal assessment

If the farmer, producer, haulier or abattoir believes they can meet the welfare standards, a formal assessment is carried out by a fully-trained Freedom Food assessor. The assessors work from a detailed checklist which corresponds to the RSPCA welfare standards.

Traceability

The assessors check that throughout the chain traceability and segregation procedures are in place to ensure that Freedom Food products do not get mixed up with non-Freedom Food products.

Meeting the standards

A farmer, haulier, processor or abattoir must meet all the RSPCA standards before they can be

accredited and become members of the Freedom Food scheme. However, a farmer cannot use the Freedom Food label on their products until they have linked up with other accredited members throughout the whole supply chain i.e. farm – haulier – abattoir.

Annual assessments

Freedom Food assesses scheme members on an annual basis. Additional visits will be made if new buildings are erected or fundamental changes are made to the building design or environment that could affect the welfare of the animals.

RSPCA independent spot checks

The RSPCA farm livestock officers' random spot check visits to scheme members help to ensure that standards are maintained at all times.

Freedom Food income

Freedom Food receives income from the scheme members, producers and retailers. As a non-profit making scheme this income is used to cover administration and operational costs only. Any profits made over and above this would be invested into farm animal welfare research.

Supermarkets

Freedom Food works closely with supermarkets to encourage them to stock Freedom Food accredited products and ensure that a wide range is available.

Price

Freedom Food products may cost a little more but for improved farm animal welfare it is a small price to pay.

Where can I get Freedom Food products?

Freedom Food is continually

Scheme progress		
	Launch July 1994	*August 2001*
Scheme members (farms, hauliers, abattoirs)	119	over 3,000
Retailers stocking Freedom Food products	400	over 6,000
Animals in the scheme	one million	approx. 19 million
Egg sales per month	100,000	82 million
Total number of animals since 1994		111 million

expanding its range of products and their availability through more retail outlets. Please see the Product Availability table below for more detailed information.

Look out for the distinctive Freedom Food logo at the following stores. Remember, if you buy Freedom Food labelled products, more shops will sell them, more farmers will produce them and more farm animals will benefit.

Product availability (as of August 2001)

Freedom Food products available (at selected stores subject to availability)

Asda
Free-range and barn eggs.

Booths
Free-range eggs, yoghurt and a range of cheeses from the delicatessen counter.

Budgens
Free-range eggs.

Co-op
Fresh free-range chicken. Fresh pork range, bacon, sausages and a range of sliced hams. Frozen omelettes. Free-range eggs.

Iceland
Free-range eggs.

Morrisons
Free-range eggs.

Safeway
Free-range, barn and organic eggs.

Sainsbury's
Columbus free-range eggs. Clarence Court eggs.

Somerfield
Free-range eggs.

Tesco
Finest free-range chicken. Finest pork range and sausages. Tesco free-range, barn and organic eggs. Columbus free-range eggs.

Waitrose
Organic eggs. Columbus free-range eggs. Clarence Court eggs.

Independents
Independent members sell a variety of products to local retailers, caterers or at farm gate.

Need to know more?

For more information about the Freedom Food scheme, its welfare standards, your nearest stockists or how to become a member of the scheme contact the RSPCA's enquiries service by e-mailing webmail@rspca.org.uk; telephoning 0870 333 5 999 or 0044 707 5335 999 for calls from outside the UK (the offices are open Monday to Friday, 9am to 5pm, when your call may be monitored or recorded for training purposes); or writing to: Enquiries Service, RSPCA, Wilberforce Way, Southwater, Horsham, West Sussex, RH13 7WN.

Please indicate your snail mail address when e-mailing as it may be appropriate to reply with copies of the Society's literature or for your request for information to be forwarded to another department. We ask that specific requests for leaflets are made in writing, accompanied by two first class stamps to cover postage.

• The above information is an extract from the RSPCA's Freedom Food web site which can be found at www.freedomfood.org.uk

© 2001 RSPCA

Suffering in silence

The RSPCA has revealed evidence of suffering on a massive scale at the heart of an industry which produces chicken – the nation's most popular meat – and is urging consumers to insist that supermarkets demand improved welfare standards from their suppliers.

A new RSPCA report – *Behind closed doors* – outlines the catalogue of illnesses including sudden heart failure, leg pain, ammonia burns and skin infections which can affect the UK's 820 million broiler chickens before they are slaughtered at just six weeks old.

Consumer role

'Consumers have a vital role to play in this campaign,' says RSPCA senior scientific officer Caroline Le Sueur.

'Shoppers can influence animal welfare standards by the food they choose and the pressure they put on retailers to demand an end to systematic cruelty. Broiler chickens typically end up having considerably less space than an A4 piece of paper to move around in – even less than the space battery hens must have from 2003, yet many consumers are unaware of the misery commonly endured by broilers.'

Behind closed doors shows how broilers now grow four times faster than egg-laying hens. This is because they are bred for maximum meat yield in the shortest possible time. To maximise growth birds are routinely given just one hour of darkness in which to rest per day and around 100,000 die prematurely each day because of the strains placed on their young bodies.

Furthermore the report states that millions experience lameness because their legs cannot bear the strain of their breast meat. With up to 50,000 broiler chickens crammed into a shed, birds also have little opportunity to move around and develop leg strength.

'In 1992 the government's own advisers recommended the introduction of legal protection for broilers and yet almost a decade later they remain the only major UK farmed animal without specific laws governing how they are reared. The RSPCA is now urging the government to take a strong lead in Europe and demand the introduction of Europe-wide protection for these animals,' says Caroline Le Sueur.

© RSPCA

Meet your meat

Information from PETA Europe Ltd (People for the Ethical Treatment of Animals)

Each year in the United Kingdom, more than 900 million mammals and birds and billions of fish are killed for food; millions more die of stress, suffocation, injuries or disease in the food industry. In his or her lifetime, the average British meat-eater is responsible for the abuse and deaths of approximately 760 chickens, 46 turkeys, 29 sheep, 20 pigs, 15 ducks, seven rabbits, five cows, one goose and more than 1,000 fish.

Down on the dairy farm

Those happy-looking cows munching grass out in the fields would tell a different story if they could speak. In order to produce milk, cows must be impregnated, but selective breeding means they now produce six to 12 times the amount of milk their calf can drink. Their udders are swollen and sore from the excess and can become infected with mastitis, which happens to about one-third of dairy cows in the EU.

Artificially inseminated while still producing milk for their calf, they can become painfully thin, and within 24 hours of giving birth, mother and calf are once again separated – a traumatic event for both. Female calves may be added to the dairy herd while males are

sometimes considered useless and are shot within days of birth.

As the mother's body wanes though over-use, she is killed when she's between 4 and 7 years old.

Dairy's connection to veal

Veal crates are banned in the UK because of their obvious cruelty. Calves are crammed into dark, wooden boxes so small that they cannot turn around. Motherless and alone, they suffer from anaemia, diarrhoea, pneumonia and lameness and see the light of day only on their way to slaughter.

Veal crates will be phased out in the EU in 2008, but veal production will remain. The only difference will be that calves will be crammed into shared pens.

The cruellest of deaths

Slaughtering in the UK is poorly governed and plagued by animal abuse. 'Murder She Wrote: The Life and Death of Farmed Animals', offered by Viva!, catalogues the abuse with scientific precision.

Cattle are frequently in-effectively stunned. Abattoir vet Gabriele Meurer explains, 'Not many animals stand still. They are all upset, some very frightened, and some move violently. The animals are never given time to calm down. Sometimes the slaughterman misses, wounding the animal terribly, instead of stunning him or her.'

Pigs are routinely conscious through the entire slaughter process. Says Meurer, 'The slaughtermen are in such a hurry that they often don't put the electric tongs in the correct position on the pigs' heads. The pigs get half or insufficiently stunned, wake up while they bleed and are obviously still alive and conscious when they are plunged into the boiling water. Sheep are stunned just as badly.'

And chickens and turkeys have it the worst of all, as they are hung upside down by their already crippled legs and routinely regain consciousness (or never lose consciousness, because of ineffective stunning) while their necks are bleeding out, thus entering the scalding tank for feather removal still conscious.

Q&A. 'Isn't slaughter regulated?'
Meat inspectors – whose job it is to

ensure proper handling and stunning of animals – focus primarily on meat hygiene. As a result, they spend most of their time in that part of the abattoir where animals are processed long after slaughter. Thus, whilst Department for Environment, Food and Rural Affairs states that there is 'robust enforcement', humane regulations continue to be flouted. Numerous studies by leading UK experts demonstrate the dramatic need for upgraded slaughterhouse standards to be established in the UK. Because of very high slaughter rates in modern slaughterhouses, it is often difficult for workers to place stunning devices on animals' heads accurately and to bleed animals effectively. Studies document that intervals between the time animals are stunned and the time they are bled are frequently too long. As a result, many pigs, sheep, cattle, calves and poultry have their throats cut while fully conscious or may regain consciousness as their blood drains from them.

Ask the experts: Gail Eisnitz, author of *Slaughterhouse*.

What happens to 'beef cattle'?

The traditional way of grazing beef cattle is in the open, although they may be wintered indoors. At about 1 year old, calves can be moved into crowded sheds and fed a high-protein diet to ensure rapid growth. Cattle must be fed antibiotics to keep them alive through the stressful conditions they're forced to endure and are in a chronic state of low-grade illness. In fattening sheds, the animals are often kept on concrete, resulting in serious leg problems. Most cattle undergo painful mutilations, such as castration and de-horning (their horns are chemically burnt off).

What happens to chickens?

The majority of 'broiler chickens' and 'laying hens' live in vast warehouses where lighting and ventilation are controlled by machines and where a system failure means widespread death. To increase profits, farmers genetically manipulate broiler chickens; as a result, most birds suffer from painful, crippling bone disorders or spinal defects.

What they don't tell you

- Labels on egg boxes are purposefully confusing. 'Farm fresh' means they were laid in the battery system; 'barn eggs' usually come from hens crammed into barns with no fresh air or daylight; even 'Freedom Foods' doesn't mean that those eggs are free-range. Often 'free-range' hens are confined to barns with 'pop holes' through which only dominant hens can access the outdoors. Regardless of their living conditions, all are slaughtered in just two years.

What happens to pigs?

More than 90 per cent of piglets are reared in overcrowded, often filthy factory-farm conditions. Lack of exercise causes pigs to become so weak that they can barely walk. They typically suffer skeletal problems and diseases of the legs and feet. Pneumonia, meningitis and dysentery are commonplace. Treated like breeding machines, they are artificially inseminated and forced to churn out five litters of piglets every two years. They are moved to farrowing crates to give birth in a barren stall with a metal contraption which separates mother from young, allowing only the necessary feeding

---

1-year-old calves can be moved into crowded sheds and fed a high-protein diet to ensure rapid growth

and not giving enough room for the mother to nuzzle her babies. After just three to four weeks, the piglets are taken from their mothers and fattened up for bacon, ham or pork. Because they get frustrated in their barren surroundings, they bite each others' tails, which causes serious wounds. To prevent this, their tails are cut off or their teeth crushed with pliers, or both, usually without anaesthetic.

- Pigs are very clean animals who take to the mud primarily to cool off and evade flies. Pigs are at least as intelligent as dogs and, like dogs, are friendly and gregarious.

How about fish?

Like other animals, fish feel pain and experience fear. Dr Donald Broom, animal welfare adviser to the British government, said, 'Anatomically, physiologically and biologically, the pain system in fish is virtually the same as in birds and mammals.'

When dragged from the ocean depths, fish undergo excruciating decompression – often the intense internal pressure ruptures their swimbladders, pops out their eyes and pushes their stomachs through their mouths. Then they're tossed on board, where many slowly suffocate or are crushed to death. Others are still alive when their throats and bellies are cut open.

Q&A. 'I don't want to give up meat. Couldn't we just treat the animals better?'

The astronomical number of animals being raised and killed for food makes it essentially impossible to treat the animals in any fashion that the average person would consider humane. Nevertheless, you should also reflect on whether you would consider it acceptable to be eaten even if someone promised to treat you better before killing you.

Ask the experts: Nedim C. Buyukmihci, V.M.D.

• The above information is an extract from PETA Europe Ltd (People for the Ethical Treatment of Animals) web site which can be found at www.petaeurope.com

Farm livestock – health and welfare

Keeping animals healthy

A healthy animal grows quickly, making the best use of the food it is given, and will produce good quality meat, milk or eggs for humans to eat and produce such as wool and leather for humans to use. A sick or suffering animal will not grow quickly so it costs more to feed. It is in farmers' best interests to make sure that the animals in their care are kept healthy throughout their lives.

Meat, milk and egg products from diseased animals are often not good enough to eat because many diseases can affect the eating or keeping quality of the food product. In some instances, it may even be unsafe to eat food from sick animals, which could be carrying disease.

To ensure that animals are kept in the best possible conditions the Farm Animal Welfare Council has issued Codes of Recommendation for each species which expand on general welfare legislation.

These Codes indicate the general aims and likely future amendments to legislation. All say 'the basic requirement for the welfare of livestock is a husbandry system appropriate to the health and, so far as is practicable, the behavioural needs of the animals, and a high standard of stockmanship'.

Animal welfare and animal medicines

The five freedoms

Farmers work to a code of five freedoms for their animals:
- Freedom from hunger
- Freedom from thirst
- Freedom from pain
- Freedom from fear
- Freedom of movement

Animals need medicines too. They suffer many similar diseases to humans. Mostly, however, they suffer infectious diseases caused by bacteria or viruses, internal parasite infesta-

tion, such as worms, and external parasites such as lice and mites. Like young children, young animals catch infectious diseases such as colds, flu and stomach bugs, and transfer parasites between themselves. Diseases can spread quickly between animals.

Because of the certainty of the transfer of disease, farmers want to protect their animals against infection. They work with their vet to build up a programme of preventative medicine for the animals. Disease causes suffering in individual animals and we should not deny them medicines which prevent or reduce their suffering or prevent them getting effective treatment.

Prevention is better than cure

For the animal, the best thing would be to prevent all illness. In many instances, animal diseases can be prevented by vaccinations.

But for many diseases, effective vaccines just do not exist. So vets have to use other classes of medicines, such as antibiotics. Nevertheless the same basic principle of prevention still applies, which is why farm animals are given antiworm treatments (anthelmintics) or coccidiostats.

Should the worst happen and disease strike a herd or flock, it is important for animal welfare that the spread of disease is prevented.

Sometimes people worry about the idea of giving animals medicines in their food or water, but there are very good reasons for doing this – often, for example, because this method involves less stress for the animals.

The law says every animal medicine must be carefully examined by independent experts before it can be licensed for sale. Veterinary surgeons who dispense medicines and animal health distributors who sell to farmers must be trained and qualified by examination. Every time a farm animal is treated, its treatment must by law be recorded, and the animal or its products (eggs or milk) may not enter the food chain until a specified period has passed following medication (the withdrawal period).

Although it is true that things like housing design and some farm management practices can affect the risk of some diseases, it is quite wrong to say that livestock would not suffer from disease if they were kept in extensive outdoor systems or in organic conditions. Infections and parasitic diseases still occur – though often for different reasons. For example most cases of salmonella in eggs have been traced to free-range systems, where wild birds have contaminated the feed and water.

Most wild animals suffer from disease and parasites.

Healthy food from healthy animals

Healthy food comes from healthy animals and there are many aspects of keeping animals well. Good stockmanship, identifying potential problems, working with the vet all play their part. But, in the interests of welfare and good food, farm animals need medicines too.

Further reading

A wide variety of material on the subject is also available from the Ministry of Agriculture, Fisheries and Food (MAFF), including Codes of Recommendation for the welfare of each livestock species. Available free from MAFF Publications, London SE99 7TP. Telephone orders 0645 556 000.

A series of briefing documents relating to the use of animal medicines on subjects such as feed additives, antibiotics, poultry medicines are available free from NOAH, 3 Crossfield Chambers, Gladbeck Way, Enfield, Middlesex EN2 7HF.

• The above information is an extract from the Food and Farming Education Service web site which can be found at www.foodandfarming.org

5 reasons for going veggie

Information from Animal Aid

1. Save animal lives

In the UK, around $2\frac{1}{2}$ million cattle, chickens, turkeys, sheep and pigs are slaughtered every day to satisfy the public's appetite for meat.

Most of these animals are reared in over-crowded factory farms where they are denied fresh air, exercise or meaningful social contact. Dairy cows are kept on a constant cycle of pregnancies to maximise milk output, and have their calves taken from them within a day or two of birth. Yet given the opportunity, farm animals are as emotionally complex as dogs, cats or other companion animals who are usually treated with more sympathy.

2. Look after your health

According to a detailed report by the World Cancer Research Fund and the American Institute for Cancer Research, 'Vegetarian groups have been shown to have lower overall mortality, lower risk of cardiovascular disease, lower rates of obesity, and longer life expectancy than general population comparison groups'.

The same report notes that a well-balanced vegetarian diet 'may decrease the risk of oral, naso-pharyngeal, stomach, pancreatic, colorectal, breast, ovarian and bladder cancers'. The consumption of animal products is also responsible for the vast majority of record levels of food poisoning incidents. Ministry of agriculture figures show that one in four pigs in the UK is infected with salmonella.

3. Feed the world

Animal farming is a massively inefficient way of producing food for people.

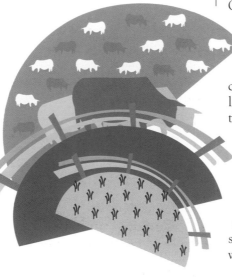

This is because animals waste most of the value of the crops they are fed in the day-to-day workings of their bodies. We can feed between four and ten times as many people on a vegetarian diet by growing crops direct for human consumption.

4. Help the environment

Animal farming is one of the main causes of water pollution in the UK – and, globally, farmed animals consume increasing quantities of precious water, land and energy.

To produce a kilo of beef protein takes up to 15 times more water than that required to produce the equivalent value of vegetable protein.

5. Say yes to life!

Choosing vegetarianism is not only a rejection of the killing of animals, it is a statement against all unnecessary violence.

To try to live our lives without causing suffering to animals is the logical extension of opposition to the persecution of humans on the grounds of race, religion, colour, or political beliefs.

You can make a difference . . . GO veggie!

• The above information is an extract from Animal Aid's web site which can be found at www.animalaid.org.uk

Animal transport

Information from the Compassion in World Farming Trust (CIWF)

Introduction

The public has been concerned about the export of live farm animals from the UK for the last 25 years. Despite years of campaigning by CIWF and others, in most years around one million lambs, sheep and pigs are exported from the UK for slaughter abroad. In recent times the concern has become so great that thousands of people, of all ages and backgrounds, in Britain and other European countries, have taken to the streets to protest about the cruelty of these long journeys and to call for an end to the suffering.

Where are animals transported?

After leaving the farm, animals may be taken to a market, slaughterhouse or another country. At markets animals are sometimes cruelly treated during loading and unloading. Sticks may be used to hit and jab animals to make them move. Markets are noisy, frightening places for animals. Some animals are sold to dealers at markets who export them to other countries. Many British sheep are exported to France and Holland. However, some British animals may be sent as far as Spain, Italy and Greece. Some of these journeys may take 40 or 50 hours or more.

What are these journeys like for the animals?

Animals are not used to being transported so the journey can be very stressful for them. Overcrowding is a common problem with animals being tightly packed together. If animals fall over they may be unable to get up and then may be trampled by other animals. In high temperatures, animals may suffer heat exhaustion and even die. Pigs in particular suffer in high temperatures as they are unable to sweat. If only a few animals are in a truck without proper partitions they may be thrown around in the lorry and suffer various injuries as vehicles brake, take corners too fast, etc. In winter, animals also suffer from the cold. Animals are very often deprived of food, water and rest on these long journeys abroad. Unloading in some continental countries can be a brutal process with animals being handled very roughly and the use of electric goads being commonplace.

How long are the journeys?

Journeys may be short if animals are just going to the local slaughterhouse, but increasingly even within the UK, journeys to slaughterhouses may be many hours. Animals travelling from the UK across Europe may travel more than 40 hours, sometimes without any food, water and rest, through varying temperature zones.

Why are live animals transported?

Most animals will be slaughtered – either straight after arrival at their destination or after a period of further fattening. Many Europeans say they prefer 'fresh' meat so they want live animals to be slaughtered in their country. Continental traders can also make a bigger profit on the meat by describing it as 'home-killed'. It is absurd that animals should be subjected to the misery of long journeys only to be slaughtered at

Despite years of campaigning by CIWF and others, in most years around one million lambs, sheep and pigs are exported from the UK for slaughter abroad

the journey's end. CIWF would like to see animals sent to slaughterhouses as near as possible to the farm on which they are reared. There is absolutely no reason (apart from profit and greed) why this could not happen. Modern vehicles with chilling facilities could then deliver chilled fresh meat throughout Europe.

Until the BSE crisis, calves were exported to be reared for veal. On the Continent calves are often kept in veal crates, a system so cruel it has been banned in Britain and will be banned in Europe; but not until 2007. The recent lifting of the ban on the export of UK beef does not apply to live animals. However, farmers are now pressing the government to get a further lifting of the beef ban which would allow the export of calves, recently separated from their mothers, to begin again. CIWF Trust believes it is doubly wrong both to export young calves on long journeys abroad and to send them to such a cruel system.

Increasing numbers of breeding sows (female pigs) are being exported to Europe. Most go from Hull or Dover to the Belgian port of Zeebrugge. CIWF investigators have trailed trucks going to a number of Belgian farms. Investigation revealed that all were keeping their sows penned individually in sow stalls so small that they cannot turn round. This is another system which has been banned in the UK on grounds of cruelty. Pigs do not travel easily. CIWF Trust believes that it is cruel to export sows to this system.

How many animals are exported each year?

In 1997 the UK exported about 539,152 sheep, lambs and pigs. The figure for 1998 was 701,202, which represents a 58% increase on the 1997 figure. These figures do not include animals exported for breeding purposes.

In 1997, 150,000 pigs were

exported for breeding purposes. In 1998 this figure increased to 180,000. Before the ban on the export of calves (due to BSE) the UK used to export approximately 500,000 calves per year.

How many animals are exported from Ireland?

In 1998, the Republic of Ireland exported 136,505 cattle and calves, 26,025 sheep, and 67,422 pigs to continental EU countries. It remains legal to export young calves from the Republic of Ireland, and in the past these have been exported to Belgium, France, Holland, Italy and Spain. Some cattle are sent on even longer journeys.

In 1996, 140,721 cattle were exported from the Republic of Ireland to countries outside the EU. Most of these went to Egypt, though Irish cattle have also been shipped to Saudi Arabia, Libya and Yemen. Trade was disrupted in 1996 when countries in the Middle East and North Africa refused to import live cattle from Ireland because of BSE fears. Strong moves are being made to re-start

What should be done?
Compassion in World Farming is campaigning for:
- animals to be slaughtered as near as possible to the farm where they are reared and only meat to be exported. In other words, the live export trade to be replaced by a carcase-only trade.
- a maximum journey limit of 8 hours for all animals being sent for slaughter or further fattening.

shipments as soon as possible; indeed, live cattle exports to the Lebanon began in late 1997. Exports in 1997 had dropped to 8,963, but rose again in 1998 to 28,703.

These animals travel on cattle boats and face a journey of a week or longer. Sometimes storms at sea are encountered and this has led to cattle dying on the boats. Between 1993 and 1995, we know that 1,202 Irish cattle died at sea *en route* to the Middle East and North Africa. This trade in live cattle to countries

outside the EU is supported by subsidies paid from EU taxpayers' money. More information about the Irish statistics can be found from CIWF Ireland's web site.

What laws protect the animals?
Under a new European Union law calves can travel up to 20 hours (with a one-hour break in the middle of the journey) before getting a 24-hour rest period. Sheep and cattle can travel for 30 hours (again, with a one-hour break in the middle of journey) and pigs can travel for 26 hours before they receive 24 hours' rest. In all cases, these are not maximum journey times because the journey can be resumed after 24 hours' rest.

• The above information is an extract from the Compassion in World Farming Trust's web site which can be found at www.ciwf.org.uk Alternatively, see page 41 for their address details.

© Compassion in World Farming Trust (CIWF)

Animal welfare

Information from the National Farmers' Union

Animal welfare standards in the UK, and the level of compliance with requirements for livestock care, are at least the equal of any in Europe.

Legislation in all aspects of animal protection – rearing on farm, transport, marketing and slaughter – is supplemented by codes of practice and professional guidance to ensure the best possible, and most appropriate treatment. Livestock keepers, and those who are closely involved with farm animals know that unless animals are humanely treated, they will not thrive.

Consumers must be confident that the food they eat is produced to the highest possible standards of safety, and under regulated animal welfare conditions. This article answers the questions that we are most frequently asked about animal welfare.

Food safety questions and answers

Q. Do farmers care about the welfare of their animals?
If you doubt that farmers care about their animals, just ask any farmer who has helped at the birth of a calf or lamb how much they care. Keeping animals is a full-time, 24-hour-a-day operation and farmers work to ensure their animals receive the best possible nourishment, shelter and veterinary care. A livestock farmer makes his living from his animals. It is therefore in his best interests to make sure they are kept in peak condition with

full attention paid to their feeding, watering, resting and exercise. A sick, suffering animal will cost more to feed, will not grow as quickly or produce as good quality meat, eggs or milk. Animal health problems can make the food product less saleable if not unsafe. So, there are many reasons why farmers care about animal welfare.

Q. So why are some animals intensively reared?
Intensive rearing normally refers to conditions where livestock are kept in large herds which tend to be kept inside for most of the year. There are a number of reasons why they are kept like this. Over the last 30 or so years, consumer pressures for cheaper foodstuffs have prompted a move towards larger farm units supplying the food processing industry with

bulk quantities of cheap, high quality milk, meat and eggs. Rearing these animals intensively in this way means that farmers can supply these quantities whilst maintaining health, hygiene and other welfare standards.

Q. What do farmers do to ensure adequate animal welfare?

Farmers know that farm animals are sentient beings in that they can, for example, feel pain, fear and fatigue. For this reason, they are committed to the humane treatment of their animals and the belief that animals have the right to the basic five freedoms at every stage of their lives. These freedoms, updated by the independent Farm Animal Welfare Council, define ideal states rather than standards of acceptable welfare. These are:

- Freedom from hunger and thirst
- Freedom from discomfort
- Freedom from pain, injury or disease
- Freedom to express normal behaviour
- Freedom from fear and distress

Q. Do animals prefer to live outside?

No, not necessarily. Research has shown that some animals prefer to be inside where the temperature is controlled, where food is brought to them, etc. Also keeping animals outside presents a range of challenges of its own. Keeping animals in extensive outdoor systems or in organic conditions does not eliminate the incidence of infections or parasitic diseases. For example, a high number of cases of salmonella in eggs has been traced to free-range systems where wild birds have contaminated the water and feed.

Q. How do farmers treat illness in their animals?

Freedom from disease is a very important component of good animal welfare. To prevent or cure disease in their animals, farmers or their veterinary surgeons will give them medicines.

All medicines given to animals are subject to strict licensing procedures by independent scientific advisers to Governments to ensure that they work, that they are safe for the animals, and will not be harmful

to the consumers of the meat, milk or eggs from the animals.

Failure to prevent or cure disease could have serious consequences not only for the well-being of the herd or flock, but also for the economic viability of the farm.

Q. Why is it necessary to transport live animals?

There will always be a need to transport farm animals, whether it be from farm to farm, farm to market or to an abattoir, either within the UK or further afield.

Since the UK is part of the European single market, the frontiers between the member countries have become irrelevant. This makes the distinction between 'domestic' and 'export' journeys a false one. For example, it may now be more financially rewarding to sell pigs to buyers

in Germany. British farmers support uniform strict welfare rules being applied fairly on all EU member states.

Q. Are there any sort of guidelines governing the welfare of animals whilst they are being transported?

Yes, there are strict regulations which livestock hauliers must follow when transporting animals.

The regulations cover vehicle standards, stocking densities, feeding, watering and rest intervals. Failure to comply can lead to hauliers losing their authorisation to transport animals. The UK's implementation and enforcement of these regulations is amongst the strictest in Europe.

• The above information is an extract from the National Farmers' Union's web site which can be found at www.nfu.org.uk

© National Farmers' Union (NFU)

Progressive farmers

Information from the Chicken 'N' Egg web site

Developments in veterinary science and in other technological areas over the past 50 years mean that poultry farmers are now able to rear birds in large, well-maintained hygienic flocks.

Improvements in the quality and nutritional value of feed now means that the birds can be fed balanced rations containing everything they need. For egg production, a high protein diet containing sufficient quantities of cereals and limestone is essential. Chickens reared for meat require protein feed with a slightly higher fat content than egg-laying birds.

Most of Britain's egg and poultry meat production is based on indoor systems. These allow the farmer to meet the birds' needs for shelter, heat, light, food and water, while being safely protected from predators and with optimum hygiene and disease control.

Great efforts are made to ensure that all birds are given enough freedom of movement. All poultry producers treat their flocks with care and attention.

For most poultry medicines, a seven-day 'withdrawal period' is required between the time when the medicine is last administered and the time when the birds are slaughtered or the eggs sent for sale to ensure that traces of medicine are not carried over to the consumer. Antibiotic growth promoters are never used for egg-laying hens, and chicken producers working under new chicken assurance scheme have voluntarily agreed to ban their use in their chicken production.

Laying hens and chickens naturally develop a 'pecking order'. This can lead to bullying which may cause injury. To avoid this, a skilled stickman may remove the tip of the upper beak, just as we trim our fingernails. This does not prevent the birds from eating or drinking.

Advances in record-keeping mean that all eggs and poultry meat produced in the UK can be traced from shop to farm.

• The above information is an extract from the Chicken 'n' Egg web site, an official National Farmers' Union web site which can be found at www.chicken-n-egg.co.uk *© National Farmers' Union (NFU)*

Factory farming

Information from the Compassion in World Farming Trust (CIWF)

Introduction

The traditional view of farming is green fields full of grazing animals, or animals lying in straw in barns, with hens scratching around in the farmyard. Sadly, this picture is far removed from the reality of life on the modern farm. The vast majority of farm animals never see the daylight or feel the sun on their backs. Millions of animals spend their entire lives in cages, stalls or huge, windowless sheds where they can barely move. The cramped conditions in which thousands of animals can be kept in one building is known as 'factory farming'.

What is factory farming?

The term 'factory farming' is used to describe very intensive forms of farming where the animals are kept in cramped conditions where they are unable to carry out their natural behaviours. The animals are treated as little more than production machines – hence the term 'factory farming'.

Which farm animals are kept like this?

Laying hens, broiler chickens, turkeys, pigs (breeding sows and fattening pigs), dairy cattle, and even fish, are usually kept in factory farm conditions.

How are hens kept?

Nearly 90% of laying hens are kept in the battery cage system for their entire lives. The cages are so small that they cannot even stretch their wings. They are unable to scratch at the ground, perch, dustbathe and make a nest. Thirty million birds are kept like this in the UK.

What about chickens reared for meat?

Meat birds are called broiler chickens and in the UK we rear over 750 million birds each year. Although these birds are not kept in cages they are still reared in very crowded

conditions. Tens of thousands of birds are crammed into windowless sheds where they are forced to grow at twice their natural rate. As a result, many will suffer bone deformities and lameness before being slaughtered at just six weeks old.

How are turkeys reared?

Most turkeys are reared in a similar way to broiler chickens. Millions of turkeys are also crammed into huge, windowless sheds. They often have part of their beaks cut off to prevent aggression. They may suffer from painful breast blisters and ulcerated feet due to standing on filthy floor litter (woodshavings soaked in turkey droppings).

How are most pigs kept?

Most breeding sows in Europe are kept in confined stalls during their 16-week pregnancy. The stalls do not allow the sow to turn around and, in some cases, sows are tethered to the concrete floor. However, thanks to CIWF, sow stalls and tethering of pigs have both been illegal in the UK since January 1999. In Britain, most sows are housed indoors in groups, though an increasing number are now kept outside. However, most of our sows give birth in a farrowing crate. The crate is narrower even than the sow stall and this makes it difficult for the sow to lie down quickly. The sow is unable to build a nest for her piglets or turn around. Young pigs are fattened in crowded conditions, often in semi-darkness with very little opportunity for movement or play.

Are dairy cows kept intensively?

Yes. The modern dairy cow is being pushed to breaking point to produce ever more milk. Most of these animals will spend the winter indoors in cubicles. Dairy cattle frequently suffer from painful mastitis (an inflammation of the udder) and lameness. The majority of male calves are still being sent to cruel veal crates in France and Holland. Many cows are worn out by the age of five or six years. Some dairy cattle are kept indoors all year round. This is known as 'zero grazing'. These cows do not graze, instead silage (fermented grass) and high protein feeds are brought to them.

In order to produce milk, the cows have to give birth to calves. Until BSE, many were exported to cruel veal crates in France and Holland. There are fears that this trade could start up again in future once the bans on the export of beef and cattle are lifted.

How are fish factory farmed?

Salmon and trout are now also

farmed in cages or pens, where they are crowded together. The cages are suspended in lakes, lochs or coastal waters. These conditions are totally unnatural and often lead to the fish becoming stressed or diseased.

How do animals suffer on factory farms?

Animals suffer in a variety of ways on factory farms. These include:

- Frustration of natural ('normal') behaviours, e.g. hens being unable to perch, dustbathe or make a nest.
- Being deprived of social contact/behaviour, e.g. isolation of sows in the farrowing crate.
- Overcrowded conditions, e.g. broiler chickens are crammed together in huge sheds and battery hens in cages.
- Physical discomfort and pain, e.g. from standing on concrete or wire mesh.
- Pushing animals to their physical limits, e.g. broiler chickens being forced to grow so quickly they suffer leg problems and dairy cattle being forced to produce large quantities of milk and being worn out in just a few years.

• The above information is an extract from the Compassion in World Farming Trust's web site which can be found at www.ciwf.org.uk

© Compassion in World Farming Trust (CIWF)

Egg-laying hens

Information from the RSPCA

After more than 30 years of campaigning for a European ban on conventional battery cages, the RSPCA can now celebrate. European agricultural ministers have voted to phase out conventional battery cages throughout Europe, although it will not come into effect until 1 January 2012.

Battery hens are kept in cages which severely restrict their movement. European Union (EU) legislation allocates only a minimum space allowance of 450 cm^2 in a battery cage for each bird. This means that each hen only has an area the size of a telephone directory to live on for as long as 12 months. There is not even enough space for a hen to stretch its wings.

Battery hens are unable to perform all sorts of natural behaviour such as nesting, scratching, perching and dust-bathing. Scientific studies show that battery hens become very stressed by living in these conditions.

New measures

From 2003 no new battery cages will be allowed to be built. A review of the situation will occur in 2005, particularly to look at the effect of the standards and relationship with the WTO.

From 2012, all conventional cages in Europe should be replaced by alternative methods such as free-range or barn production. Producers can, however, continue to keep birds in enriched cages which provide nesting and perching facilities – although the RSPCA does not consider these to be viable alternatives and they may not significantly improve welfare.

The RSPCA is delighted by a recent decision to label all eggs produced in the EU with clear, concise information about the method of production. At present, eggs do not have to be labelled with their production method. For many years, consumers have been confused by terms such as 'farm fresh' and 'country fresh' used to describe eggs produced in battery cage systems. The Commission has decided that, from 2004, egg packs must bear the terms 'free-range eggs', 'barn eggs' or 'eggs from caged hens'.

However, the RSPCA is very concerned that the Commission has also decided to increase the stocking density outdoors for free-range hens, from 1,000 birds per hectare to 2,500 hens per hectare. With more than

Battery hens are kept in cages which severely restrict their movement

double the number of hens occupying the same amount of land, it will become much more difficult to manage the pasture area, and maintain adequate grass cover.

Freedom Food

In the UK the RSPCA's Freedom Food scheme has led the way in establishing high minimum standards for the keeping of laying hens. Freedom Food standards insist that hens are not kept in cages and are given enough space to allow them to behave naturally. At present, over 82 million Freedom Food trade-marked eggs are sold every month in the UK.

If you are a UK consumer, you can help until the ban becomes effective by buying only eggs from free-range or barn systems accredited to RSPCA Freedom Food welfare standards.

If you are an EU citizen, you can help by writing to Commissioner Fischler, DG Agriculture, Rue de la Loi 200, Brussels, B-1049, Belgium, to ask him to introduce a mandatory egg labelling scheme.

If you live elsewhere in the world, why not ask your government about the size of this problem in your country.

• The above information is from the RSPCA's web site which can be found at www.rspca.org.uk Alternatively, see page 41 for their address details.

© 2001 RSPCA

Pig welfare

Information from the RSPCA

Millions of pigs across the European Union (EU) live in conditions that cause severe stress and suffering. The RSPCA is taking part in a Europe-wide campaign to improve EU legislation on how farmed pigs are kept.

Pigs have many of their ancestors' instincts and are social, highly intelligent, inquisitive animals. But EU law allows many different systems for keeping pigs – most offer just a barren, crowded environment with no bedding for comfort or recreation.

Around 20-30 per cent of breeding sows in the UK live in free-range conditions which, when properly managed, can give pigs a high quality of life. The remaining 70-80 per cent are kept in indoor group housing systems.

However, most sows in other European countries are forced to live on concrete or slatted floors, in stalls too narrow for them to turn around throughout their four-month pregnancies. Sometimes they are tethered to the floor by a short chain. The use of both stalls and tethers, both now banned in the UK since 1999, causes severe welfare and health problems. Tethering, but not stalls, will be banned in Europe from 2005.

Welfare-friendly alternatives operate successfully in several countries including the UK. Indoor sows are kept in groups with space to move around and bedding for comfort and rooting.

Confining crates

The RSPCA also wants the use of conventional farrowing crate systems phased out. Modern, farmed sows have at least two litters a year of up to 14 piglets each. Most indoor sows give birth in farrowing crates that aim to protect piglets from crushing but that also stop the sow turning around. Sows are confined for three to four weeks after giving birth until their piglets are weaned. Farrowing crates are extremely restrictive and the absence of bedding in many crate systems prevents pregnant sows nest-building.

Alternative farrowing systems for indoor sows are already used on some farms in several EU countries. These may confine sows for just a few days around farrowing, when piglets are at their most vulnerable, or give them complete freedom throughout. Outdoor sows have their young in individual, well-bedded farrowing arcs from which they can come and go freely.

Welfare-friendly foods

Consumers of pigmeat products need clear and informative labelling to make informed choices. If compulsory labelling is introduced, welfare-conscious consumers can buy pork products knowing the animals have been reared to certain standards. The RSPCA has its own farm animal welfare food labelling scheme – Freedom Food.

An EU Directive lays down minimum standards for the protection of farmed pigs. Some member states, including the UK, have already implemented national legislation that surpasses the Directive in certain areas. Denmark, Finland and the Netherlands recently passed new welfare laws which will come into effect in the next few years. But the laws of many EU countries merely implement the Directive's minimum requirements.

The European Commission proposed changes to the Directive early in 2001 to change the way in which Europe's pigs are kept.

RSPCA position

The RSPCA called for:
- a Europe-wide ban on sow stalls
- a ban on conventional farrowing crates, except for the first few days
- the provision of bedding and rooting material at all stages of production
- sufficient space for pigs and prohibition of fully-slatted floors
- a ban on castration and a prohibition on the routine use of other painful practices, except on veterinary advice
- trained and competent pig stock-keepers
- clear and informative labelling.

The Council of Ministers' decision

The Ministers agreed to implement the following changes:

- A Europe-wide ban on sow stalls – but not until 2013
- Provision of rooting material – but only for breeding sows
- Provision of a solid lying area – but only for breeding sows
- Requirement for welfare-focused training for all pig stock-keepers
- No changes to use of conventional farrowing crates – recommended that more research is needed.

The Europe-wide ban on sow stalls is much to be welcomed. However, the RSPCA believes that the phase-out period is unnecessarily long, and will mean that millions of sows across Europe will continue to suffer in narrow, barren individual stalls for many years to come. The Society is also extremely disappointed that many of the other provisions it called for, such as a ban on conventional farrowing crates except for a few days round farrowing time, have not been adopted. The requirement for stock-keepers to be properly trained, and for rooting material and high fibre food to be provided to sows, are positive moves, but growing pigs will not benefit in any way with respect to more space or provision of bedding/rooting material.

Discussions are continuing in Europe on some other issues such as castration and tail-docking, with a decision expected shortly.

Take action

- If you are a UK resident write to the Secretary of State, Rt Hon. Margaret Beckett MP, at the Department of Environment, Food and Rural Affairs, Nobel House, 17 Smith Square, London SW1P 3JR. Express disappointment at the Council of Ministers' decision, and urge her to press for a total ban on castration, and on other practices such as tail docking unless on specific veterinary advice, during ongoing discussions on these issues in Europe. Also ask that the UK presses for compulsory provision of both more space and rooting material for growing pigs.
- If you are an EU resident, write to the European Consumer Protection Commissioner, David Byrne, at European Commission, 200 Rue de la Loi, 1049 Brussels, Belgium. Press him to introduce tighter controls on practices such as tail docking, and to ban castration. Let him know your concerns about the failure of the EU to make further improvements in the welfare of pigs. You can also write to your MEP.
- If you live elsewhere, ask your government what they are doing about this issue. An RSPCA report – *The welfare of pigs* – and a leaflet – *A captive life* – are available from the RSPCA Enquiries Service.

• The above information is from the RSPCA's web site which can be found at www.rspca.org.uk

Pork adverts are banned in 'welfare friendly' row

By David Brown, Agriculture Editor

Advertisements urging consumers to buy 'welfare friendly' British pork and bacon instead of meat from allegedly sub-standard foreign farms were banned yesterday by the Advertising Standards Authority.

The four advertisements, which claimed that pigs in this country enjoyed better conditions than animals abroad, were part of a £4.6 million Government-backed newspaper campaign run by the Meat and Livestock Commission last summer to boost sales of British meat in the face of cheaper imports.

The campaign responded to protests from farmers that they were being driven out of business by low prices and statutory health and welfare costs not imposed on other European Union producers. But the authority ruled yesterday that the advertisements, which upset vegetarians, animal welfare campaigners and European competitors, were misleading and contained claims that could not be substantiated.

Juliet Gellatley, the director of the Vegetarians' International Voice for Animals, one of the groups that complained to the ASA, said: 'The MLC boasts of high welfare standards yet never shows the public the real conditions in which these intelligent animals are forced to live.'

The commission lodged an immediate appeal with Sir John Caines, the ASA's independent reviewer, in an attempt to have the ruling overturned.

ADDITIONAL RESOURCES

You might like to contact the following organisations for further information. Due to the increasing cost of postage, many organisations cannot respond to enquiries unless they receive a stamped, addressed envelope.

Animal Aid
The Old Chapel
Bradford Street
Tonbridge, TN9 1AW
Tel: 01732 364546
Fax: 01732 366533
E-mail: info@animalaid.org.uk
Web site: www.animalaid.org.uk
Animal Aid campaigns against all forms of animal abuse and promote a cruelty-free lifestyle. Produces information including their quarterly magazine *Outrage*. To receive information on an issue, please send a large sae to the address above.

British Nutrition Foundation (BNF)
High Holborn House
52-54 High Holborn
London, WC1V 6RQ
Tel: 020 7404 6504
Fax: 020 7404 6747
E-mail: postbox@nutrition.org.uk
Web site: www.nutrition.org.uk
The BNF is an independent charity which provides reliable information and advice on nutrition and related health matters. They produce a wide range of leaflets, briefing papers and books.

Compassion in World Farming Trust (CIWF)
Charles House
5a Charles Street
Petersfield, GU32 3EH
Tel: 01730 268070
Fax: 01730 260791
E-mail: ciwftrust@ciwf.co.uk
Web site: www.ciwf.co.uk
CIWF seeks the abolition of inherently cruel practices to live animals for slaughter. Publishes information including a series of factsheets called *Farmfacts* on various issues.

The Dairy Council
5-7 John Princes Street
London, W1G 0JN
Tel: 020 7499 7822
Fax: 020 7408 1353
E-mail: info@dairycouncil.org.uk
Web site: www.milk.co.uk

The Dairy Council, founded in 1920, is the co-ordinating body for the dairy industry's generic information and promotion activities in Great Britain. It is funded by dairy farmers via the Milk Development Council and by processors and manufacturers via the Dairy Industry Federation.

Meat and Livestock Commission (MLC)
PO Box 44, Winterhill House
Snowdon Drive
Milton Keynes, MK6 1AX
Tel: 01908 677577
Fax: 01908 609221
Web site: www.mlc.org.uk
The MLC supports the marketing of British meat and livestock, offers support to farmers and others in the meat and livestock industry, and promotes training and research in the meat industry.

National Farmers' Union (NFU)
164 Shaftesbury Avenue
London, WC2H 8HL
Tel: 020 7331 7200
Fax: 020 7331 7313
E-mail: nfu@nfu.org.uk
Web site: www.nfu.org.uk
The NFU is the democratic organisation representing farmers and growers in England and Wales. Its central objective is to promote the interests of those farming businesses producing high quality food and drink products for customers and markets both at home and abroad.

PETA Europe Ltd (People for the Ethical Treatment of Animals)
PO Box 3169
London, SW18 4WJ
Tel: 020 8870 3966
Fax: 020 8870 1686
E-mail: info@petaeurope.org.uk
Web site: www.petaeurope.org
Targets animal abuse in laboratories, in the fur and meat trades, and in the entertainment industry. Produces a range of factsheets and leaflets.

Royal Society for the Prevention of Cruelty to Animals (RSPCA)
Wilberforce Way
Southwater
Horsham, RH13 9RS
Tel: 08700 101181
Fax: 01403 241048
Web site: www.rspca.org.uk
The RSPCA is a charity and the world's oldest animal welfare organisation. The Society can be found just about anywhere the welfare of animals is at stake.

The Vegan Society Ltd
Donald Watson House
7 Battle Road
St Leonards-on-Sea, TN37 7AA
Tel: 01424 427393
Fax: 01424 717064
E-mail: info@vegansociety.com
Web site: www.vegansociety.com
Promotes ways of living which seek, as far as possible and practical, to exclude all forms of exploitation of animals for food, clothing or any other purpose. The society produces magazines and factsheets.

The Vegetarian Society of the United Kingdom Ltd
Parkdale, Dunham Road
Altrincham, WA14 4QG
Tel: 0161 928 0793
Fax: 0161 926 9182
E-mail: info@vegsoc.org
Web site: www.vegsoc.org
The Vegetarian Society is working towards its vision of a future where the vegetarian diet is acknowledged as the norm.

Viva!
12 Queen Square
Brighton, BN1 3FD
Tel: 01273 777 688
Fax: 01273 776755
E-mail: info@viva.org.uk
Web site: www.viva.org.uk
Viva! launches regular, hard-hitting campaigns and has forced the vegetarian and vegan debate back on to the agenda – on TV, radio and in the Press.

INDEX

abattoirs, and animal welfare 25, 26, 28
acne, and milk consumption 18
advertisements
    for British meat 4
    pork and bacon 40
age, and heart disease, and vegetarian diets 20
anaemia, and iron deficiency 5
animal welfare
    and vegetarianism 6, 24-40
    see also livestock farming
antibiotics, and farm livestock 32

babies, weaning and iron in the diet 5
bacon, vegetarian 21, 22
beef cattle 31
BSE (bovine spongiform encephalopathy), and the
    transportation of live animals 34, 35, 37
burgers, vegetarian 2, 21, 22

calves, and veal production 30, 34, 37
cancer
    and diet 7, 15, 16
    COMA report on 4
    dairy products 18
    and meat consumption 8, 15
    and milk consumption 17
    and vegetarian diets 19
cattle
    beef cattle 31
    dairy cows 17, 18, 30, 37
    transportation on cattle boats 35
    veal production 30, 34, 37
chickens
    egg production 36
    battery system 37, 38
    living conditions 31, 36
    poultry production 36, 37
    slaughtering 30-1
    welfare issues 25
children
    anti-milk campaign directed at 17, 18
    and iron deficiency 5
    and vegetarian diets 1
cholesterol
    and coronary heart disease 10, 19
    and egg consumption 16
    and vegetarian diets 15, 20
coronary heart disease (CHD) see heart disease
cows, and milk production 17, 18, 30, 37

death, from heart disease, and vegetarianism 20
diets see vegetarian diets
disease
    and diet 15, 19
    prevention and treatment of farm livestock 32-3, 36
drinks, vegan 14

eggs
    free-range 31, 33, 36, 38
    labelling on egg boxes 31
    production 36
    battery system 37, 38
    and the RSPCA Freedom Food Scheme 28
    and vegan diets 12, 16
environment, and vegetarianism 6-7, 26, 27, 33
European Union (EU) legislation
    on battery hens 38
    on pig welfare 39-40
    on the transportation of live animals 35, 36

factory farming 24, 30-1, 35-6, 37-8
    and animal suffering 38
families
    of vegans 11, 12
    of vegetarians 11
Farm Animal Welfare Council 24, 36
    Codes of Recommendation 32
farmers
    and animal welfare 35-6
    and the anti-milk campaign 17
fat in the diet
    reducing 10
    vegan diets 14
fish
    environmental effects of fishing 7, 27
    farming 7, 37-8
    health benefits of eating 20
    health risks of eating 16
    pain system in 31
food
    and the RSPCA Freedom Food Scheme 27-9
    see also meat consumption; vegetarian food
food poisoning, and animal products 3, 7, 16
foot-and-mouth disease, and vegetarianism 22

genetically modified (GM) foods 7
girls, and vegetarian diets 1
global warming, and livestock cultivation 6
Government policies, health strategies and healthy eating
    4-5

health benefits, of vegetarian diets 15, 20, 26, 33
health risks, of animal products 16
healthy eating
    and meat consumption 4-5, 8, 10
    and vegan diets 12
    and vegetarian diets 7, 9, 20
heart disease
    and meat consumption 15
    and milk consumption 17, 18
    and vegetarians 7, 8, 16, 19, 20
high blood pressure (hypertension), and meat
    consumption 15

human evolution, and meat consumption 5

iron in the diet 3, 5, 8

lacto-ovo-vegetarians 1, 6
lacto-vegetarians 1
life insurance scheme for vegetarians 19
livestock farming
  and animal welfare 24-40
  abattoirs 25, 26, 28
  auction markets 25-6, 34
  European Union legislation on 35, 36, 38, 39-40
  and factory farming 24, 30-1, 35-6, 37-8
  farm buildings 25
  and the 'five freedoms' 24, 27-8, 32, 36
  keeping animals healthy 32-3, 36
  and milk production 17, 18, 30, 37
  pigs 25, 26, 39-40
  slaughtering 30-1
  transportation of live animals 25, 34-5, 36
  UK legislation on 24-5, 35, 36
  and the environment 6-7, 26, 27
  pigs 25, 26, 31, 34, 37, 39-40

macrobiotic diets 1
meat consumption
  cooking meat 8, 10
  and fat 10
  health risks of 3, 8
  and healthy eating 4-5, 8, 10
  and iron 5
  meat-based diets 15
  storing and freezing meat 8
men, and vegetarianism 1
milk
  anti-milk campaign 17, 18
  and lactose intolerance 18
  and vegan diets 12, 16

nutrition
  and fruitarian diets 1
  and macrobiotic diets 1
  and meat consumption 5
  and vegan diets 12, 13-14
  and vegetarian diets 3, 9

osteoporosis, and dairy products 17, 18

pigs
  exported to Europe 34
  factory farming 31, 37, 39
  transportation of live 34
  welfare issues 25, 26, 39-40
protein in the diet
  excess 15-16
  vegans 13, 16
  vegetarians 9

strokes, and diet 18
supermarkets, and the RSPCA Freedom Food Scheme
  28, 29

teenagers see young people
turkeys, factory farming of 37

vaccinations, for farm livestock 32
veal production 30, 34, 37
vegan diets 1, 6, 12
  alternatives to animal products 12, 13
  costs of 14
  drinks 14
  famous vegans 12, 13
  and nutrition 12, 13-14
  and protein 13, 16
  and teenagers 13-14
vegetarian diets 1
  giving up 23
  health benefits of 15, 20, 26, 33
  and healthy eating 7, 9, 20
  lacto-ovo-vegetarian 1, 6
  lacto-vegetarian 1
  macrobiotic 1
  and nutrition 3, 9
  protein in 9
  semi or demi vegetarian 1
  vegan 1, 6, 12
vegetarian food
  characteristics of 6
  cooking 2, 11
  eating out 2-3
  foreign 2
  market value of 21
  meat substitutes 2, 21-2
  pulses 2
  ready-made foods 2
  sauces and gravies 2
vegetarians
  and animal welfare 6, 26, 33
  becoming a vegetarian 11
  defining 2, 6
  and the environment 6-7, 26, 27, 33
  and foot-and-mouth disease 22
  and heart disease 7, 8, 16, 19, 20
  iron-rich foods for 3, 8
  life insurance scheme for 19
  percentage of in the population 1, 21
  resistance from family and friends 11
vitamins
  in milk 18
  and vegan diets 12, 14
  and vegetarian diets 9

water supplies, and livestock cultivation 7
women
  iron deficiency in 5
  and vegetarianism 1

young people
  and iron deficiency 5
  and vegan diets 13-14
  and vegetarian diets 1

Zen macrobiotic diets 1

ACKNOWLEDGEMENTS

The publisher is grateful for permission to reproduce the following material.

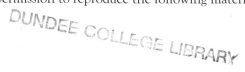

While every care has been taken to trace and acknowledge copyright, the publisher tenders its apology for any accidental infringement or where copyright has proved untraceable. The publisher would be pleased to come to a suitable arrangement in any such case with the rightful owner.

Chapter One: A Question of Diet

Vegetarian and vegan diets, © British Nutrition Foundation (BNF), *Live and let live*, © Viva!, *The role of meat in a balanced diet*, © Meat and Livestock Commission (MLC), *UK meat industry data*, © Meat and Livestock Commission (MLC), *Food survey*, © Meat and Livestock Commission (MLC), *A few basic facts*, © The Vegetarian Society of the United Kingdom Ltd, *Meat in the diet*, © British Nutrition Foundation (BNF), *Vegetarian nutrition*, © Animal Aid, *Vegetarian food sales*, © Mintel 1998, *Meat and fat*, © Meat and Livestock Commission (MLC), *Meat and fat*, © Meat and Livestock Commission (MLC), *How to be a vegetarian in ten easy steps*, © Source Unknown, *Vegan FAQs*, © The Vegan Society, *Teen vegans*, © The Vegan Society, *Nutrition or know your onions!*, © The Vegan Society, *Eating for life*, © PETA Europe Ltd (People for the Ethical Treatment of Animals), *Number of vegetarians*, © Realeat Polls 1994-1998, *Vegetarians*, © NOP Poll for Seven Seas and The Vegetarian Society, *Farmers condemn anti-milk campaign aimed at children*, © Telegraph Group Limited, London 2001, *The Dairy Council*, © The Dairy Council, *Vegetarians offered discount offer*, © Guardian Newspapers Limited 2001, *Vegetarians and heart disease*, © The Coronary Prevention Group, *Protein*, © The Vegetarian Society of the United Kingdom Ltd, *Cheat meat*, © Guardian Newspapers Limited 2001, *Animal culls 'turning people into vegetarians'*, © Guardian Newspapers Limited 2001, *Welcome return to pleasures of flesh*, © Guardian Newspapers Limited 2001.

Chapter Two: Animal Welfare

Animal welfare, © Food and Farming Education Service 2001, *Go veggie*, © Viva!, *Animals and the environment*, © The Vegetarian Society of the United Kingdom Ltd, *Freedom food*, © 2001 RSPCA, *Suffering in silence*, © 2001 RSPCA, *Meet your meat*, © PETA Europe Ltd (People for the Ethical Treatment of Animals), *Farm livestock – health and welfare*, © Food and Farming Education Service 2001, *5 reasons for going veggie*, © Animal Aid, *Animal transport*, © Compassion in World Farming Trust (CIWF), *Animal welfare*, © National Farmers' Union (NFU), *Progressive farmers*, © National Farmers' Union (NFU), *Factory farming*, © Compassion in World Farming Trust (CIWF), *Egg-laying hens*, © 2001 RSPCA, *Pig welfare*, © 2001 RSPCA, *Pork adverts are banned in 'welfare friendly' row*, © Telegraph Group Limited, London 2001.

Photographs and illustrations:

Pages 1, 11, 19, 24, 39: Pumpkin House, pages 6, 8, 12, 17, 20, 30, 32, 37, 40: Simon Kneebone.

Craig Donnellan
Cambridge
January, 2002